MEDLARS

In memory of Jenny
1950 – 2005

THE ENGLISH KITCHEN

MEDLARS

GROWING AND COOKING

JANE STEWARD

PROSPECT BOOKS

2023

This edition published in 2023 in Great Britain and the USA by Prospect Books at 26 Parke Road, London, SW13 9NG

Text © 2023, Jane Steward
Illustrations on pp. 2, 24, 90, 120 © 2023, Ave Design Studio

British Library Cataloguing in Publication Data:
A catalogue entry for this book is available from the British Library.

ISBN 13: 978-1-909248-77-9

Printed by Short Run Press, Exeter, UK.

FSC
www.fsc.org
MIX
Paper from
responsible sources
FSC® C014540

CONTENTS

PREFACE

This is the story of my medlar life. I'm grateful to Prospect Books for inviting me to write about growing and cooking medlars for its English Kitchen series. This book will sit alongside its companion volumes on quinces, damsons, and cherries and mulberries.

I would have been pleased to discover a book like this when I was newly acquainted with medlars, and looking for essential information on growing and getting the best out of this mysterious fruit. I hope you're happy to have found it too. This forgotten fruit deserves to be more widely recognised and appreciated for its beauty in the garden, for its unique flavour on the table, and its nutritional benefits.

I still wonder when I would have collided with medlars, if I hadn't met and then fallen in love with David in late 2008. Before long I was introduced to the medlar tree tucked away in a corner of his Cambridgeshire village garden. I was mystified by the graceful, arching, autumnal specimen heaving with open-faced, golden brown and golf ball sized fruit. We stood there together, lush damp grass under our feet, sheltered by the unexpectedly benevolent and arching boughs of the tree which reached out above our heads. We left the surprisingly still very hard medlars on the tree for the following weekend, and neither of us gave them any more thought.

It wasn't immediately obvious to me how we could use these odd-looking fruits. David had not been in the habit of picking and using them either. A week later, on our return from a busy time in London, we were disappointed to see that all the fruits had disappeared, and it didn't occur to either of us to scrabble around in the long grass and gathering mass of leafy debris where they were almost certainly lurking. We simply and wrongly assumed that they had been taken by the birds or squirrels.

The twenty-year-old tree had been given to David by his father, in memory of his late grandparents. His nan was a Suffolk countrywoman who had access to a medlar tree at the village house where she worked. She made medlar jelly for her husband to eat with his regular afternoon meal of bread and cheese when he came in from the fields. We first heard this part of the story a couple of years ago from cousin Fred, their oldest grandson, who'd happily spent part of his school holidays with Nan and Grandad Steward at their home on the banks of the River Orwell.

By the following autumn, David and I had committed to making a life together. An excited townie, embracing the novelty of a rural dimension to my life, I kept an eye on the medlar tree as the season unfolded. Honestly, I still knew nothing about these weird looking, rock-hard fruits. We gathered up the windfalls hiding among long grass and the fallen autumnal leaves (a reliable sign that medlars are ready to pick) and plucked the remaining ones from the tree. They were useless in this state, that was obvious, absolutely impossible to break into. Looking back, I don't recall how we learned that they had to be 'bletted', whatever that was. David probably looked it up online. I carefully laid them out in a single layer on wooden trays in the greenhouse where I hoped they would soften to the point where we could use them somehow or another. This 'patient waiting' stage was bletting, the scientific exchange of a tannic, inedible hardness for a sweet, soft and juicy texture. Along with these most desirable changes, bletting causes a near total loss of pectin and a dramatic browning of the flesh. Inevitably, having set them aside to blet, I nearly forgot about them. I returned to them two or three weeks later, no harm had been done and they were much darker, very soft and sweetly fragrant. It didn't occur to me to try one 'au naturel' now that they were bletted. Although I was an enthusiastic home cook, I wasn't and had never been a jam or marmalade maker, so I had to work out how to use them. I suspected that it wasn't going to be straightforward making something of and with these squish-balls, but I did want to have a go.

I found an ancient sounding 'receipt' for medlar cheese somewhere on the internet. It involved lemons, cloves, muscovado sugar and water. Simmering these ingredients together in the only giant pan I owned, a tall-sided pasta pot, for a ridiculously long time, produced a liquid mass after I had sieved it as instructed. The strained result required a second simmer. The pan was the wrong shape altogether, with too little surface area to volume. My first mistake. After what seemed like ages, the volcanic contents had thickened slightly. It wasn't a great success, but it tasted pleasant enough. Fruity, delicately spicy, with a hint of citrus and a definite autumnal base note, I could imagine eating it with a crunchy cheddar. I decanted some into glass ramekins and set them to chill in the fridge. This first attempt at a 'medlar cheese' was politely received that Christmas. We ate some of it with Stilton. Months later, these little pots were still in remarkably good shape, lurking in the fridge.

As a wholly inexperienced maker of preserves, I had been put off the Nigel Slater recipe for medlar jelly, which is still available on the *Guardian* website, as I didn't own a jelly bag and stand. And the bletted medlars' lack of pectin, which I was warned about, was daunting. This time I didn't have a go.

That was that, I thought, and my interest switched to the trees. Having seen David's established medlar tree in flower, I was enthusiastic about the young one we were given as a wedding present when we married the following year, in 2010. This 'wedding tree' was carefully dug up by me and transplanted to our Norfolk home when we relocated two years later. We took on six acres when we made this move, much of the area away from the house was rough grass and fenced into discrete paddocks. David was very excited about the additional space, his previous home nestled in a two-acre plot. My terraced garden in London's East End measured four metres by five. I don't think I fully engaged in the responsibility we were acquiring. I was very taken by the house itself, especially the kitchen with its double doors onto the garden, a sink large enough for bathing a baby, and a dark green Aga. We went for it.

I envisaged an avenue of medlar trees gracing a sheltered spot just beyond a hawthorn hedge, set halfway up the garden. It would delight us with white blossoms in the late spring and be followed by stunning ornamental gold and red foliage in the lead-up to Christmas. The annual crop of medlar fruit barely crossed my mind.

Alongside the medlars, a fruit cage was built in memory of my grandfather. We filled it with transplanted autumn raspberries, added the morello cherry tree my daughters had given me for my fiftieth birthday, sourced gooseberry bushes and lastly some strawberries. These and the nearby rhubarb, elderflowers and their berries, as well as wonderful veteran Bramleys in the old orchard were quite enough to be getting on with around my existing business commitments.

In December 2012, our first winter at Eastgate, the children helped us plant nine additional medlar trees, a generous birthday present from my mum, along with our 'wedding tree'. We were putting down our own roots in this new place. I slowly familiarised myself with the basics of preserve making, relying initially on Darina Allen's reassuring tones and clear guidance in *Forgotten Skills of Cooking* for successful marmalade, elderflower cordial, raspberry and strawberry jams. Volumes on preserve making by Pam Corbin, Beryl Cook and others found their place on the bookshelves.

In early 2015 I had just completed a complex and satisfying four-year coaching project, heading up a great team of coaches who were working individually with the inspirational leaders of an NGO. While I contemplated my next professional move, life took an unexpected turn. I was quickly and successfully treated for an asymptomatic cancer which had been picked up by a relatively new screening programme at the Norfolk and Norwich University Hospital. My recovery was enormously helped by time spent in the garden, with my hands in the soil. I raided the freezer stash of home-grown berries and apples, and whiled away happy hours in the kitchen, experimenting with recipes and preserving the results in jars. In this, I was occasionally accompanied by my youngest daughter who also wanted to learn more about the art of making jam.

I was amazed at the restorative power of gardening and preserve making, literally shifting me from my head into my hands. David and my girls observed that I was thriving, relishing the exploration of these new avenues, and they were right. This was an essential time of personal transition, which enabled me to close the door on my twelve-year career as an executive leadership coach and business owner. It meant the end of the week-in, week-out commute to London, and I flung open the doors to my Norfolk life. I wanted to embark on something new and exciting, as yet unclear. I felt both energised by possibilities and tremendously unfocused.

There was a very modest stash of medlars in the freezer, the earliest sign that the medlar avenue was establishing itself. Recipes were now a bit easier to find, and I gathered together Nigel Slater's 2010 piece from the *Guardian*, and researched medlar jelly recipes by Jane Grigson, Pam Corbin and Diana Henry to try out. The medlar itself was still in my peripheral field of vision. When I made my first batch, I was amazed at the two-stage transformation of the soft, brown fruits into glistening, softly set, tawny or ruby coloured jelly. It was magic, the ultimate preserve making alchemy. I was gently hitching myself to this mysterious fruit, feeling my way with it. I soon understood that medlars won't be rushed. Time and patience are the unnamed essential ingredients when working with them, which may have partially contributed to their slide from view during the twentieth century.

I experimented with both bletted and unbletted fruit, these fully grown hard ones being packed with pectin. I tried out varying quantities of lemon juice depending on the proportion of hard fruit I was using. Medlar jelly made entirely of these is a beautiful straw colour and sets like a dream. Its downsides are that it has virtually no depth of flavour and its dry, tannic character dominates. One hundred percent soft, dark fruit makes a delicious jelly, however my early results were sometimes unpredictable. Slow to set, due to the lack of pectin, the unavoidably lengthy boiling time made it slightly chewy. On other occasions the stuff remained unaccountably runny. I pondered on how much sugar was really necessary to create the best flavoured and textured result, and the all-important keeping qualities. I was never tempted to use preserving or jam sugar. It was definitely worth persevering. Medlar jelly is jewel like, a tawny or ruby colour, with a hint of citrus following the initial subtle sweetness that complements cheeses, furred and feathered game, charcuterie, terrines, parfaits and all meat other than beef. The recipe I now use is on p. 137.

Medlar fruit cheese recipes were trickier to track down. I adapted those I found for quince, damson and apple. David was very keen on this set purée of the fruit pulp when I made my first batch and then another. It wasn't intended to be a sliceable product, more like a paste, and he loved it spread on hot granary toast. I felt that I had put my sloppy 2009 efforts firmly behind me.

I was determined to produce something worthwhile with the few medlars I had. While this was going on, my eldest daughter was researching companies devoted to producing medlar products. There are a couple of very well-known ones which make a wide range that included medlar, Wilkins of Tiptree and Tracklements in the West Country for example, but there was no dedicated, single fruit specialist. Was this a real gap that needed to be filled? I wasn't sure that a hard-to-source seasonal fruit would generate enough interest in Norfolk to sustain a business, even a very small home-based one. Would it be possible to create any interest further afield?

I still knew very little about the fruit or the trees, but I did have a growing desire to create something tangible and enduring that signified to me that I was still here. If it was to be a medlar focused enterprise, we would need to plant more trees because the fruit is unbuyable in any quantity, even in the season. And if I was going to give this a go, I needed access to a reliable, sustainable and increasing volume of medlars. Planting an orchard appealed because it would be beautiful and useful, a unique addition to my new home county. Adding more medlar trees would increase the diversity of our own plot, which we had coincidentally discovered was a fruit farm in the early twentieth century, with hundreds of Bramleys, pears and an underplanting of blackcurrants. We'd started fostering honey bees, and Simon Greenwood, a local bee farmer whose grandfather had given him his first hive of bees as a ten-year old, cheerily named it a 'bees' banquet' when he came to meet us and see what we were doing. For David and me, as a couple, the medlar truly held an emotional significance by this time and David was enthusiastic about the whole idea of an orchard. He was also ace at digging the planting holes.

Having an idea is only the first of many steps for a new venture. Could I actually make and sell products that people would love enough to buy them regularly? Would people be interested in the story of the medlar? I knew nothing about how pricing worked, as a maker or from a retailer's perspective. I had so much to learn. We bought more trees that autumn and I registered Eastgate Larder Limited in late 2015. My middle daughter, a print graphic designer, took me on the brand journey, and thanks to her and a colleague, this embryonic business soon had a visual identity and a website. Hand-drawn images were commissioned for the labels, and small, elegant, straight-sided jars were chosen to reflect the scarcity of the fruit. They nestle nicely in the hand, and look good enough to put straight on the table alongside a cheeseboard.

As I had some frozen medlars from our original avenue of ten trees I made some stock to sell on my first outing as a maker at Norfolk's Aylsham Show in August 2016. Clare Buxton, the longstanding steward of the show's food and drink producers' tent, had visited the orchard earlier in the year and, unbeknownst to me, she had generously allocated me a front row spot in the traditional canvas marquee. I decided to bring a couple of young medlar trees in pots for visitors to see what they look like. Armed with an order book, tasting jars of jelly and fruit cheese as well as a few to purchase, it was a good day. A first conversation with my neighbouring stallholder and now a good friend, Sarah Pettegree, owner and creator of Brays Cottage pork pies, encouraged me to think beyond my self-limiting ambition to use only Eastgate grown medlars. I came away with the immediate challenge of locating additional medlar fruit in Norfolk to be harvested that November. This would see me through the first full year of production while my youthful, albeit substantially expanded orchard established itself. Eight locations were found and permissions secured. A Twitter introduction from Norwich restaurateur and 2015 winner of the Great British Menu, Richard Bainbridge, led me to a coastal greengrocer where 'a few medlars' (100 kg it turned out) awaited me, bundled into plastic bags and cardboard boxes. I was told they'd come from a man called Bill, but nothing more. The following year I was able to see the two beautiful semi-reclining trees in his walled garden at Sheringham Hall which had produced this amazing haul, and which kindly repeated the performance that autumn. The business model was now clear: Norfolk grown medlars would be blended with Eastgate's fruit in every batch. Fruit generously given is recognised through charity donations by reference to their weight. This model appealed to the lengthening list of garden owners who have contributed their fruit in successive years.

I've got to know, and I continue to meet, so many supportive garden owners who have planted a medlar in memory of someone dear, or simply because they love the quirky year-round beauty of the tree. Medlar trees are often found growing at National Trust properties, sometimes as a singleton as at Blickling Hall, or in a pair as at Oxburgh. The twin medlar trees at Holkham Hall are in one of the walled garden rooms, adjacent to the rows of white Solaris and red Regent grape vines. I carefully harvest this fruit each year to make a pure Holkham blend medlar jelly which is sold in their gift shop. I'm still unsure which medlar cultivar is planted here, and unfortunately there are no written records to steer me. Judging by the behaviour of the fruit at harvest and bletting time,

I wonder whether they might be 'Westerveld', but I couldn't swear to it. My own 'Westerveld' medlars also like to be picked late and they blet slowly.

Medlars from Norfolk gardens within fifteen miles of multi award winning Flint Vineyard, which nestles among Norfolk's south facing slopes in the Waveney Valley, are made into medlar jelly for their 'fifteen-mile lunch' boards and for sale in their shop. Here it is paired with Jonny Crickmore's Baron Bigod and Julie Cheyney's St Jude cheeses, both made with the milk from the Fen Farm based herd of Montbéliarde dairy cows. This red pied breed originates in the Bourgogne-Franche-Comté region of eastern France. Charcuterie is supplied by Marsh Pig. This valuable partnership with Flint's winemaker Ben Witchell and his award-winning wines is a wonderful showcase for medlar jelly.

A strategy was emerging: I needed to raise awareness of the fruit, encourage people to plant a tree, try the fruit or a medlar preserve. I could see that this might appeal to some people. But what about beer drinkers, art lovers, gin fans? A medium-term plan to find collaborative ways to bring about a beer, a gin, and make some art was taking shape for later.

The following year I was accepted as a monthly stallholder at Norfolk's highly regarded and popular Creake Abbey Farmers' Market, frequently ranked among the top twenty in the country. It was convivial in the straw barn, catching up with fellow producers and sharing news and stories, as well as being a place to meet enthusiastic supporters and buyers of all kinds of locally produced food and drink. Occasionally a medlar afficionado visited my stall expressly to buy, but more often these were opportunities to introduce the fruit and offer tastings. Norfolk cheeses and local charcuterie went on to my tasting boards, one of which was the rotating circular piece of slate, complete with Eastgate Larder branding, along with the jelly and fruit cheese. The soft, bloomy dairy cheeses to go with medlar jelly or a beautiful blue to partner with the medlar fruit cheese frequently led to sales. There seemed to be an appetite for something different, a novel cousin of the apple, pear and quince which was also full of history.

This market is a popular destination for regional fine food shop owners looking for new products. This, together with a couple of sales trips around East Anglia and further west into Shropshire and Wales (where Sarah and I were warmly hosted overnight by Barrie and JoJo Thomson, then owners of The High Street Deli in Newtown), and a burgeoning social media (especially Instagram), were instrumental in the establishment of a loyal band of independent businesses wishing to stock medlar products. This list includes the Norfolk Deli in Hunstanton, with its views down to the sea. The owners, Mark and Rosie Kacary, also offer online shopping which includes a comprehensive Norfolk farmers' market, enabling hundreds of artisan Norfolk made food and drink products to reach customers anywhere in the UK. Mark says:

> Jane's love and passion for the medlar has resulted in our ability to offer our cheese loving customers a local, historic alternative to the classic combination of cheese and quince. The medlar's delicate but distinctive flavour is the perfect accompaniment to a fully flavoured locally produced cheese, such as a Baron Bigod or even a Mrs Temple's Binham Blue. Beautifully presented, you can always find it on our cheeseboard alongside a few more robust local chutneys to offer a variety of flavour combinations and alternatives.

By 2020 the Eastgate medlar orchard was 120 trees strong. It comprised nine individual cultivars, including a substantial number of the 'Nottingham' which I have found to be excellent for preserve making. I invited Janet Sleep, the chair of the Norfolk group of Plant Heritage, the world's largest plant conservation charity, to visit the orchard in the summer of 2018. She encouraged me to send in a proposal and with her support I finally submitted my full application for National Collection status in the winter of 2019-20. Just as the pandemic took hold, the orchard was granted my wish. It is Norfolk's first arboreal collection and it is available to visitors.

In early 2022 I restarted the medlar talks and tasting events I offer to gardening clubs around the county. These came about as a result of my only outing as a stallholder at the Royal Norfolk Show in 2017. Jane Dalton introduced herself as the secretary of Great Hockham gardening club near Wymondham. Would I like to give a talk about the medlar to the club members later that year? Having made a career out of avoiding PowerPoint presentations and all that they entail, I cheerfully said I would. If it was OK with her, I would treat it rather like a conversation about the history, growing, and ways of using medlars, bringing tasting jars as well as a few for people to buy if they wished. As it was October, I chose some individual fruits off my own trees to take with me. They and their leaves were closely examined. Jane is a brilliant gardener and an equally talented artist; the following week I received a framed watercolour of the medlars I had left behind after the talk.

The range of medlar products I make has evolved. I've refined and improved my own processes, discovered what sells best and what has a smaller reach. The medlar fruit cheese, while delicious, is sadly unviable commercially and I've stopped making it. The maximum batch size is less than half that achievable for medlar jelly (the best seller by far) and it takes slightly longer as I rely on gentle dehydration to set the fruit pulp, sugar and a splash of lemon juice into a paste. It's tough deciding to drop a product, but it has been the right decision for me both commercially and emotionally. And I no longer get scalded by volcanic eruptions of molten fruit pulp.

I introduced a limited edition spicy medlar chutney in 2018 which sells out every year. The recipe is adapted from one in Pam Corbin's *River Cottage Preserves Handbook*, the key difference being a much greater proportion of medlar than apple. I use our Bramleys and chillies grown just down the road from here. I'm having a go at growing the garlic too.

The road to launching Norfolk Medlar Gin Liqueur in 2021 was bumpy. The unexpected cloudiness, volume and low abv issues I discovered in early 2019 were finally resolved following a chance conversation with a Corsican maker of fruit liqueurs, Marie Paule. She had handed the four of us a mystery glass of what turned out to be her own gorgeous quince liqueur at the end of a wonderful meal at her restaurant. Correctly guessing it was a quince liqueur gave me an opening to mention my frustration with the medlar and ask her some gritty questions. A small test batch of medlar gin that autumn confirmed her advice.

The base is Jonathan and Alison Redding's superlative Norfolk Gin, the county's first artisan gin. Norfolk Gin is known as 'the gin with music in', an essential accompanying ingredient while they make the gin, fill and label their distinctive ceramic bottles. We were introduced to one another by Sarah P. Our growing friendship has helped me navigate the stop and start stages of this product's development. Norfolk Gin's citrus and cardamom notes embrace the medlar during the lengthy steeping process, producing a less alcoholic (just under 30% abv) result which is good to drink neat as an accompaniment to a slice of Nigella Lawson's lemon and elderflower drizzle cake. It makes a great cocktail with sparkling wine, and is a refreshing gin and tonic with a twist of lime and a sprig of thyme. It is also pretty good served over ice with a slice of orange.

Newly harvested fruit goes to Wildcraft Brewery (www.wildcraftbrewery.co.uk) in November for brewer Mike Deal to craft into a few hundred litres of medlar beer. We met as neighbouring event stallholders in the early days of our respective businesses. Foraging for ingredients is key to his brand offering. This year he has barrel-aged a quantity of medlar beer in whisky, brandy and port casks. The results are amazing, in both flavour and abv. Delicious with a cheeseboard too.

Soon after starting out, we were at a gathering hosted by an artist pal of ours where I met Mary Blue, an American artist now resident in Norfolk. She spent time in our orchard painting our 'wedding tree' through the seasons. The vibrant energy she brings to her interpretation of the medlar is beautiful. Her work can be seen at www.maryblue.co.uk

Each of these relationships and connections form the threads which have gradually woven themselves magically into a network of kindness, talent and expertise which continue to enrich my life and enable Eastgate Larder to thrive. At the heart of this is David, our kids and grandchildren. And Norfolk.

Introduction

Together with mulberries and quinces, medlars (*Mespilus germanica*), are often described as 'forgotten' fruits. They are less well known than apples and pears, cherries and plums, they never appear in supermarkets and are rarely, if ever, sold by greengrocers.

Their story goes back around three thousand years. Medlars grew wild between the Caspian Sea and the Black Sea, where they attracted human attention. They meandered slowly west in the company of Greeks, and northwards across Europe probably in the company of Romans. They turned up here, as a luxury food perhaps, during the centuries-long Roman occupation of Britain.

The medlar's image in Britain has long been defined by its looks (not beautiful) and it has acquired a few graphically descriptive nicknames along the way: 'dog's bottom' and 'monkey's bum' to name but two. The Anglo-Saxons appreciated their qualities as health remedies, and the Georgians and Victorians liked them as a winter fruit. By the end of the First World War, they were drifting to the edge of awareness, and they'd all but disappeared from view by the turn of the twentieth century.

They Can't Ration These is a 1940 cookery book, written by Vicomte de Mauduit. It was regarded as a survival guide for the British. Food rationing had been introduced in January of that year, and by June the threat of invasion was real. Medlars didn't make the cut, despite their potential usefulness, especially during the cold months.

The extent to which medlars had faded from our memory during the twentieth and into the twenty-first century, was further emphasised in a 2018 survey of traditional British foods. The aim was 'to determine the conservation status of twenty-four foods that tend to be associated with (the) olden days'. Less than a tenth of the two thousand people who participated said they had eaten medlars in the past. It is encouraging that nearly a quarter of respondents said they'd be willing to try these previously unknown fruits. Bee Wilson, author and food writer, estimates that a similar proportion of adults have an extreme or irrational dislike of anything new or unfamiliar especially in relation to foods. I accept this, however I'm also optimistic that boosting awareness of the medlar and offering different ways of presenting it is the first step to tempting people to taste it. That's been my experience in Norfolk and London. The colour, flavour and texture of medlar jelly help to make it an accessible and tasty entry point for new consumers.

The medlar's twenty-first century revival is building momentum from a very low base. Influential food writers and restaurateurs champion them in the season. They have been appearing in British agroforestry farm schemes for a couple of decades. A farmer near Abergavenny is planting 300 medlar trees in two phases; he intends to use the fruit commercially for an alcoholic drink as well as making medlar jelly and fruit cheese.

Recent scientific research studies conducted at universities in Turkey, Romania and Poland report on a nutrient and mineral rich fruit, packed with vitamins, polyphenols, minerals and fibre. This is an attractive mix of attributes for the dietary-health aware among us.

Helen Allen's painting of the medlar, which graces the cover of this book, was commissioned by my husband David for my sixtieth birthday. Helen is an internationally renowned botanical artist, who was the owner and principal of the Chelsea School of Botanical Art, based in the Chelsea Physic Garden, from 2014 until 2018. We were invited to visit her at her studio where she talked me through her months' long process, working exclusively with live material, including some from Eastgate. Helen's painting perfectly illustrates the ornamental beauty of medlars through the seasons: the tightly budded promise of creamy white flowers precedes the summer of growth for the fruit culminates in a crescendo of rich, mellow and autumnal finery. Her painting has greater depth and texture than any photograph I've seen, inviting me to reach out and feel each component, perfectly conveying the long-awaited arrival of the flowers, the texture of the leaves and, of course, the fruit. She captures the harvest-ready fruit so vividly I'm transported to the tree, where in my imagination, I breathe in the cool, misty air, and I am swept up in the sensation of lightly crushed leaf fall muddled with floppy damp grass, as the orchard slows itself down towards the arrival of winter.

The fruit's nickname, both amusingly and crudely, makes it the butt of jokes. While this might be a handy way to accurately identify a medlar, it creates a somewhat unbalanced view of the trees and their crop. Yes, it is a quirkily shaped fruit whose form has long inspired the vernacular: 'openarse', 'dog's bottom, 'monkey's bum', to name but three. A touch of crudity might make medlars unforgettable to some. When they are fully grown, ripe and ready to eat, some dismiss them as rotten, not ripe. That feels a bit harsh.

To my mind, they become soft, fragrant and sweet yet citrussy.

What about the word 'medlar', which has given us various spellings over the centuries: meddeler, meddler, medle, medler among others. These convey a sense of 'to have sexual intercourse'. 'Openarse' graphically refers to the fruit parts surrounded by the calyx lobes. The French colloquially use my favourite term *'cul de chien'*, which ensures that *Mespilus* medlars are never muddled up with *Eriobotrya loquats*, also called *'la nèfle'*.

The medlar, *Mespilus germanica*, is a member of the vast rose family, *Rosaceae*, and is a first cousin of the apple, pear and quince. Like them, medlar fruit grows on a tree which at maturity, say twenty years old, will be wider than it is tall. Fruiting wood is at least a year old and appears in the form of short spurs, which bear creamy white, five petalled flowers around a mass of yellow stamens in the late spring. These are set against a backdrop of bright, tapering leaves, almost velvety to the touch, which will have unfurled several weeks earlier. Pollinators of all kinds love the flowers. Landing pads for honey bees is how I think of them. A single tree is productive (they are parthenocarpic, meaning they can develop fruit without prior fertilization), and when it has set, the fruit is visible from early summer onwards. It grows on, largely undisturbed by pests, and fattens up in readiness for the last of the seasonal fruit harvests from early November. Physically the fruits measure between three and six centimetres (1 ½ to 3 inches) in diameter when fully grown, depending on the cultivar. They have the colouring and skin texture of a darkened russet apple, with a pleasingly rough and matte exterior.

With the exception of one cultivar, the 'Iranian', edible ripeness of medlars involves bletting the fruit, most often off the tree. This natural process replaces the astringent, tannic, hard flesh with dark, soft, fragrant and sweet flesh. It occurs over a few days or weeks, depending on two factors: when the fruit was picked or fell to the ground and the prevailing temperature. If you're not already familiar with the flavour, a fresh, perfectly bletted medlar tastes like a date that has sucked on a lemon, as described by Niki Segnit, author of *The Flavour Thesaurus* and *Lateral Cooking*.

Its flesh surrounds five inedible stones which encase the seeds. The texture of the sweet flesh is slightly grainy, like pears some say, and it has a mildly astringent finish. Others liken the flavour to a slightly spiced apple sauce, ripe figs, guava or honeyed apricots. Take your pick among these descriptions, medlars are good to eat as a table fruit, accompanied by a glass of wine and some cheese.

The RHS website lists several medlar cultivars. The most user-friendly and widely available is the 'Nottingham', an open-faced small to medium sized fruit. Well flavoured and nicely textured as a fresh table fruit, it also makes excellent preserves. Nottinghams often feature a characteristic and harmless fissure, as seen on the book's cover, which helps me to correctly identify them.

The 'Large Dutch' is quite popular in gardens, it has larger leaves and produces fruit of about two inches diameter. It is not quite as finely flavoured eaten fresh, but is very useful in preserve making. The 'Common Dutch' is smaller and round, and very similar in behaviour to the 'Nottingham'.

'Flanders Giant' and 'Royal' have been included in agroforestry plantings together with the 'Nottingham'. Both are good to cook with and perform well in beer making.

'Breda', 'Bredase Reus', 'Macrocarpa' and 'Westerveld' are medium sized, round and useful in preserve making. The 'Westerveld' is distinctive because it is the last to harvest, usually in early December. Any earlier and the bletting is hard and slow work.

The 'Iranian' deserves a special mention, as I think it is the very finest for eating as a table fruit. It is narrower and longer than the others with a closed calyx. It's highly distinctive. It was developed by Keepers Nursery in Kent to fully blet on the tree and offer you a 'freshly picked fruit' eating experience in the first half of November.

Last but not least there is the 'Large Russian', up to three inches across. It isn't great as a fresh fruit, but works well in a preserves-making mix.

Other cultivars listed on the website are so-called synonym varieties. Finally, the 'Sibley Patio Medlar' deserves a mention because of its compact tree form, making it ideal for the smallest setting.

Another of the medlar fruit's quirks is that it is brown after it has fully bletted. Bletted simply means that the fruit is sweetly ripe and ready to eat. I'm definitely someone who finds profound joy in brown food: chocolate, a deeply fragrant winter soup, a richly aromatic braise of beef, one of David's perfect cups of coffee. However, we've been schooled differently when it comes to fruit, and anything with a brown tinge is often, but not always, a sign of some less than optimal freshness or overripeness. A brown-black banana skin indicates flavour encased within, perfect for that easy teatime loaf baked with vine fruits which have plumped in a splash of orange juice. In a medlar, the dark hue represents flavour, texture and readiness. To my mind brown is a credible and desirable colour for a fruit which symbolises the autumn and winter months. This said, some people are unswerving in their belief that the very best way of using bletted medlars is on the compost heap. Each to their own.

The world is now ready for the medlar to be the focus of a book. My aim is to create a useful and informative resource for ornamental gardeners, orchardists and cooks alike, a book about growing and cooking medlars, with tips on cultivating them as well as recipes to try out. The bibliography lists all the sources which have been referred to in the course of writing. Medlars are increasing their fan base in North America, in Australia and New Zealand, so I've included some cultivar and tree nursery information for these readers too.

I've long visualised the book which I had looked for in 2008 when I first met David's medlar tree in the garden of his Cambridgeshire home. I hope it appeals to all sorts of readers: the simply curious, keen cooks, and completists who already have this imprint's companion books on damsons, quinces, and cherries and mulberries. I've included some horticultural and culinary history to place the medlar in its context together with thoughts on choosing and growing medlar trees, where I draw extensively on my own experience. Likewise, the ups and downs of using them in the kitchen. People who've had dealings with medlars often remind me that they can be a less than straightforward fruit to work with, and I don't always disagree with them. As you may have read in the Preface, I've confronted these challenges myself and I am more than happy to share my experience and ways to smooth out the wrinkles when you're working with them.

Thanks to the timing of this book, three research papers, all published in 2021, have contributed up-to-date findings on the medlar's nutritional merits as well as current and potential nutraceutical uses of the fruit. The medlar has probably been appreciated for its therapeutic qualities, as well as its dietary usefulness, for around three thousand years. A group of Italian researchers published their scientific paper in 2019 which looked at genetic diversity among medlar cultivars, considering their agronomical, pomological and qualitative traits. They are supportive of the medlar's potential role in nutritional medicine, and they highlighted the ease of medlar cultivation on poor soils, and the fruit's pleasant taste.

The history of *Mespilus germanica* is still somewhat mysterious, and I'm grateful for Baird and Thieret's 1989 paper on the medlar, which I have referred to in several places and is listed in the Bibliography. There are traps for the unwary hidden along the twists and turns of internet alleyways which can, and do, lead to a dead end. I've endeavoured to avoid such hazards. A degree of uncertainty surrounds the medlar's true geographical origins and the fruit's route to England. It is possible that wild medlars grew around three thousand years ago along the western shores of the Caspian Sea, roughly in the area of what is now Iran and Azerbaijan. We suspect that, possibly with the help of humans and assisted by animals, they gradually moved westward through Greece via the Roman Empire into Northern Europe and finally across the English Channel. The little brown fruits borne on the original wild medlar, an undomesticated thorny bush, must have proved themselves to be of some value to humans for them to have migrated over such a distance. We know, thanks to modern scientific research, that the medlar is a useful source of vitamins, fibre and minerals, not just a naturally sweet treat. Our early ancestors may have discovered their usefulness and flavour through trial and error, just as they would have done with many other plants.

The arrival of medlars on these shores can't be precisely fixed; it is possible that the Romans were instrumental in bringing them here at some time during their occupation. They introduced, among other fruits and vegetables, figs, grapes and mulberries, asparagus and artichokes, spices and some herbs. Why not the medlar too? It looks as though inhabitants or visitors to the Roman centre that developed around the earlier Iron Age settlement at Silchester, Hampshire, were consumers of medlar fruit. Some fortunate archaeological finds, specifically two medlar stones in a drain, were revealed and identified 120 years ago. Could these stones have originated in an 'exotic' import, brought here by individual soldiers who had a taste for medlars? It is entirely possible. More than this, the idea of a soldier's tunic pockets containing a few medlars feels and sounds compelling. If they were brought in by individuals rather than commercially, I can't believe that every single medlar stone would have been meticulously disposed of after eating. In my imagination I hope that medlar trees may have grown here and there as a result of seed falling from the fingers or being spat out, eventually growing among a cluster of other trees, in the wild or on common land. Aside from its medicinal merit, I am sure that the fruit would have been a useful food source during long winters.

Centuries later, towards the first millennium, they are mentioned in Anglo-Saxon documents, both as medicaments and as food. It is in the early medieval period that we find the first, clear records of productive, cultivated and carefully nurtured medlar trees growing in England. Unless they'd been intentionally grafted onto rootstock, these would have started life as pretty slow growing naturally seeded trees. Grown from a seed, they would take a while to reach fruiting maturity, at least fifteen to twenty years, whereas a grafted tree is productive within three or four years. What is clear is that this member of the *Rosaceae* family became successfully naturalised in the British climate, as did their close pome fruit cousins the apple, the pear and the quince.

This early part of the story unfolds quite slowly. By the sixteenth century the medlar was being planted in orchards, and the fruit was highly sought after on the English table, favoured as a fashionable delicacy. The higher echelons of society embraced medlars, perhaps inspired by Henry VIII who received gifts of them and ate them on court occasions, and they were included in the orchard gardens planted at Hampton Court Palace. Elizabeth I's reign brought about a significant horticultural evolution in the late sixteenth century and continuing into the early seventeenth century: kitchen gardens were laid out and orchards were highly fashionable, flowers selected for their medicinal attributes were beginning to be appreciated for their beauty too. New books on cookery and husbandry, written in English, sold well to an increasingly literate population. The vogue for growing and cultivating embedded itself in our culture and horticulture became a competitive sport, which continues to this day.

Early seventeenth-century records tell us of named medlar cultivars being bought directly from growers in the Low Countries for the orchards that were being laid out in grand domestic settings. These would have been high quality trees and difficult, if not impossible, to source here. By the nineteenth century, varieties of *Mespilus germanica* with 'enlarged and eatable fruit' were commonly growing in gardens in the south of Britain, and were regularly brought to market in the autumn, including to London's Covent Garden. The range of fruit and vegetables eaten was far broader than it is today, and included some delicacies such as medlars and bullaces, which would have been served at the table of Queen Victoria.

Why did the medlar fade into obscurity during the twentieth century? There's no simple explanation for its decline in popularity. The increasing affordability of sugar in England as the nineteenth century gave way to the twentieth may have played a part in it gradually disappearing from view, despite the best efforts of epicurean and wine connoisseur George Saintsbury. He summed up the medlar in *Notes on a Cellar*, published in 1920:

> …the one fruit which seems to go best with all wine, hock to sherry, claret to port is the medlar – an admirable and distinguished thing in and by itself and a worthy mate for the best of liquors.

It continued to be a regular, if less frequent, feature of the winter diet until around a hundred years ago. The medlar's sweetness may partly explain why it was popular at a time when sugar was extremely costly. Its usefulness as a winter fruit is undoubted. There may also have been a continuing appreciation of its usefulness as a health remedy. It is tempting to fix on a single reason for the decline, but it is more likely that a combination of socioeconomic and demographic factors conspired against it. The nation's changing appetite was an inevitable response to advances in refrigerated transport, which may have contributed to the fruit's gradual slide from view over several decades. Similarly, the increased availability and affordability of exotic and otherwise luxury seasonal fruit has displaced some of our homegrown produce. The annual ritual of domestic jam making and preserving of abundant harvests to ensure variety during the winter has felt less necessary as a wider range of produce of all kinds is readily available to buy. Domestic refrigerators and freezers appeared in our homes and accelerated us into the modern age of shopping and food retail. Shopping these days often means a weekly supermarket trip, not a daily visit to the butcher, baker and greengrocer. In the post-war period orchards and hedgerows were grubbed up to accommodate farmers' larger, more efficient and mechanized fields. Market gardens, once a significant source of fresh produce for the home market, were out-competed by growers in Spain and the Netherlands. Importing fruit and vegetables became bigger and bigger business.

Despite the generally industrialised feel of the modern food sector, shoppers continue to take an interest in new and unusual sounding products. Consumers enjoy meeting and talking with small-scale producers, hearing the story or inspiration behind a cheese or preserve at a farmers' market or a food festival. The network of independent food shops in the UK selling a range of hand-picked, carefully curated, small production food of all sorts continues to expand, albeit at a slower rate. As a group, we are content for our products not to be on a supermarket shelf or in their chiller cabinet, which matters to the independent stockist. It is still business, of course, but I like to think that the wholesale independent customer relationships we build can feel like a partnership. We work hard to look after them. They, in turn, look after you, the individual customer.

Medlars were never grown in any quantity in commercial British orchards, not even in their heyday. They would have mainly been the province of the domestic garden or orchard, a walled garden in a grander or ecclesiastical setting. They didn't turn up in hedgerows either, even though they would have thrived in this setting. There seems to have been some historical cultural resistance to the idea that opportunities to forage wild fruit could have been a positive contribution to the diet and health of a rural population. These days, medlars are mostly unbuyable in the UK, which further contributes to the general lack of awareness of this underutilised fruit.

If your interest is piqued, the surest way to include medlars in your diet is to plant a tree of your own. I promise, they are easy to grow, even in a pot, and require virtually no pruning. They will crop in their third year after planting. Happy in a pair or as part of a group, a medlar tree will also thrive on its own. They are frost hardy and self-fertile, relatively disease and pest free, even pesky wasps and squirrels ignore them. Once the roots are down, a half-standard medlar tree produces anywhere between five and ten kilos of fruit by its tenth birthday, an elegant sufficiency for personal consumption and sharing with friends and family.

There are several food writers who enthusiastically share their medlar recipes in the autumn months. Nigel Slater is well known for his personal affection for medlars. He grows them in his garden and cites the medlar as his favourite fruit jelly. His 2010 *Observer* article describes bletting and goes on to give his recipe for making the preserve to serve with roast pheasant. The article is searchable online and well worth reading.

Medlars are worthy of our attention, with more to offer than meets the eye. I hope that this book will encourage you to seek them out, try the fruit, maybe make some medlar preserves and, if you have the space, plant a tree of your own.

The Story of the Medlar

The medlar's story is a gentle journey through time and across continents. It took many centuries and thousands of miles to make its way from the shores of the Caspian Sea to England. It became the favourite fruit of an English king and appeared in the plays of Shakespeare, before falling from favour in the twentieth century. It is now enjoying such a revival that there is a Plant Heritage National Collection of medlar trees in the UK and they are being planted at the National Arboretum in Washington DC.

The Fashionable Medlar

If the medlar had a golden age in England, it was probably between the sixteenth and eighteenth centuries. Interest in medlars tracked the burgeoning Tudor enthusiasm for growing a wider range of fruit, and establishing kitchen gardens. Royalty was probably at the vanguard of this trend, and it is King Henry VIII who helped the fruit to become fashionable and consequently more widely available in orchards and at the table.

John Chapman, head gardener at the king's recently acquired

Hampton Court Palace, laid out the royal home's new orchard in the early 1530s, to the north of the old gardens. It was planted with fruit trees such as medlar, pear, damson, cherry and apple. These varieties were not only beautiful, they didn't require any special conditions to produce a crop. *The Book of Apples* confirms that royal example 'helped to stimulate consumption in fashionable circles', which in turn led to the establishment of new orchards to supply the metropolis in the sixteenth century. It is entirely credible that King Henry's taste for medlars may have helped to popularise the fruit in the upper echelons of society. A note of expenses paid in November 1531 from the privy purse to the palace's head gardener reveals that a sum of seven shillings and sixpence was disbursed for a quantity of 'peres and medelers' to be delivered to the king's table.

The newly fashionable medlar was drafted in to help resolve the great matter that preoccupied the monarch in the early 1530s, namely the lack of an heir. In late 1532, King Henry took Anne Boleyn across the English Channel to meet King Francis I, with the intention of enlisting the French king's help in his frustrating efforts to secure a papal annulment for his marriage to the devout Catherine of Aragon. Despite the king's largesse in Calais, where the English entertained the French in some style, he was unsuccessful. Among the sumptuous supplies of swans, geese, capons, ducks and larks were large quantities of medlars. One list, to satisfy and entertain the two kings and their parties on four separate occasions, included 400 dozen pears and the same of medlars. Another list also included large quantities of medlars, apples and pears.

Just as her father had, Queen Elizabeth I adored gardens. The Elizabethan court went into the countryside each summer, hosted for a few weeks at a time by local nobility. In case she should decide to visit any one of these noble families, by way of preparation they created ever more lavish and complicated planting schemes in their gardens, orchards and on their estates to impress and entertain her. This added a competitive edge to their enthusiasm for planting orchards and kitchen gardens which continued into the seventeenth century.

In the first decade of the new century, John Tradescant the Elder became head gardener to Sir Robert Cecil, the first Earl of Salisbury, at Hatfield House in Hertfordshire, where Queen Elizabeth had spent part of her childhood. Cecil had already obtained medlar, quince, walnut and cherry trees for his garden from a Low Countries grower, Henrich Marchfeld. During 1610 and 1611, Cecil sent Tradescant across the North Sea to buy more stock. The gardener kept an account of his purchases and expenses, from which we can see what he bought and where. His journey took him by ship from Gravesend to Flushing in the Netherlands, in early autumn, and he travelled on from there to Leiden, via Middleburg, Rotterdam and Delft. Here in Delft, nurseryman Dirryk Hevesson sold him several varieties of fruit trees including 'two great medlar trees' for four shillings, and 'two great medlar trees of Naples' for five. It is fairly certain that Tradescant wouldn't have travelled all this way to buy any plants or trees that could have been easily obtained in England. This story underlines the increasing reputation of Dutch growers and nurserymen.

Mea Allen, writing in the 1960s in her first major work of horticultural history, says that 'These entries of costly fruits and plants are therefore valuable records of first introductions to this country', and she suggests that this would have been a very early record of the great medlar tree of Naples, 'evidently our large Dutch medlar.'

If, however, it had been the same 'medlar of Naples' which had been described in John Gerard's herbal of 1597, later to appear in John Parkinson's books of 1629 and 1640, it is more likely to have been the azerole. (The azerole is another fruit-bearing member of the hawthorn family, also a relative of the medlar, which bears golden fruit and is native to southern Europe.) The 'great medlar trees' referred to may have been what we now call the Dutch variety, but there isn't a more detailed description in Tradescant's account.

The turn of the sixteenth and seventeenth centuries coincides with the first performances of Shakespeare's plays which mention the medlar: *As You Like It, Romeo and Juliet, Measure for Measure,* and *Timon of Athens.* None of the quotes are at all flattering. They talk of rottenness before ripeness, a rotten medlar, open-arse and in the last of these plays, Timon, having retreated in solitude to a cave, rejects the offer of a medlar to sustain him. Shakespeare may have been expressing his own views of the medlar, or making fun of their continuing popularity at court. Whatever he had in mind, they provided him with a useful and graphic metaphor.

The appeal of the medlar extended beyond the large estates into the domestic arena well into the eighteenth century. In his diary entry for 6 January 1785, the Reverend James Woodforde, the 'Country Parson' of Weston Longville in Norfolk, related that Mr Dade of nearby Mattishall had brought him some medlars from Mr Smith, the vicar of that parish.

The Medlar's Origins

What do we know about the medlar's origin as a species, where was its natural homeland, what was it about it that attracted humans, and made it interesting and valuable to them, how did it make its way here, and what evidence is there of its arrival and cultivation thereafter?

We think we can date the ancient and mysterious story of the medlar back to around 1000 BCE. Although we don't precisely know where medlar trees first grew in the wild in their bushy, thorny and undomesticated form, we believe that they were relatively abundant in and around Iran, the Caucasus, Crimea, south-east Balkans, Greece, southern Bulgaria, northern Turkey, Georgia, Armenia, Azerbaijan and Turkmenia (modern day Turkmenistan). This broad sweep of territory lies to the north of the Fertile Crescent, the cradle of diverse plant and animal species and early farming practices.

Aside from their value to humans as a food source, it is possible that the first communities to embrace the pome fruit family in their natural home 3000 years ago may also have been among the first to experiment with them for medicinal or remedial reasons. In a fruit beauty contest, the medlar brings up the rear when compared to its prettier pome relatives, the apple, pear and quince. Imagining for a moment what might have tempted the first consumers of these funny-looking medlars, I wonder whether it was discovering their ability to help relieve possibly life-threatening digestive complaints, including diarrhoea. The fully grown, hard medlar has binding powers. It is unpalatable and nearly impossible to bite into, especially so for someone feeling poorly. I wonder whether it may have been cooked in water, which breaks open and softens the flesh. The resulting milky coloured astringent liquid may have done the trick. Conversely, a constipated digestive system could have been eased by the consumption of sweet, ripe and bletted medlar fruit.

HOMELAND

The medlar's original home is much better understood thanks to the research done by four scientists during the middle years of the twentieth century: Nikolai Ivanovich Vavilov, P.M. Zukovskij, Kasimierz Browicz and Dr V.A. Evreinoff. Those of you who have come across the article by botanists J. R. Baird and J. W. Thieret,

'The medlar (*Mespilus germanica, Rosaceae*) from antiquity to obscurity', published in *Economic Botany*, will be familiar with what follows.

In the 1930s Vavilov, a botanist and geneticist, described eight 'centres of origin' of cultivated plants. One of the oldest of these is the Fertile Crescent, where in his view different kinds of indigenous plants first grew. He placed *Mespilus germanica* in the interior of Asia Minor, Transcaucasia, Iran and Turkmenistan.

Research undertaken by P.M. Zukovskij in 1950 suggested that:

> *Mespilus germanica*, in spite of its name, occurs wild in the Caucaus and the southern Crimea, northern Iran, Asia Minor, the Balkan peninsula and Greece. Wild forms found in Turkmenia are probably escapes. The greatest form of diversity is found in Talys in Azerbaijan, where it occurs at almost all altitudes […] The plant was obviously domesticated in this area in ancient times.

A separate study by the eminent Polish botanist Kasimierz Browicz expanded contemporary thinking about the medlar's original geographical reach. He thought that its 'true homeland' was spread across the south-east of the Balkan Peninsula, Asia Minor, the Caucasus, Crimea, northern Iran and possibly Turkmenistan. Careful analysis of literary writings and evidence in herbariums supported his view.

In his own work, Browicz had referred to a significant presence of wild medlars in the stretch of land between the Black Sea and the Caspian Sea. The respected botanist Dr V.A. Evreinoff, whose name was later given to a large medlar cultivar goes further still. Writing in 1953, he confirmed Browicz's view about a vibrant concentration of wild medlar existing between the two seas, saying that the medlar

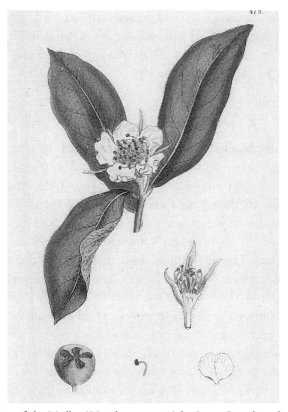

Illustration of the Medlar (*Mespilus germanica*) by James Sowerby, taken from *English Botany or Coloured Figures of British Plants*, published by Hardwicke in 1863.

may have originally been cultivated along the north-western shores of the Caspian Sea, the land-locked body of water encircled by Turkmenistan, Iran, Armenia, Russia and Kazakhstan around three thousand years ago.

I have to mention that Browicz's opinion about the medlar's origins was cast in doubt in the 1970s, when medlar leaf impressions were discovered in Burgtonna, East Germany. This site dates back to the Last Interglacial period, between 130,000 and 115,000 years ago. The Burgtonna leaf impressions don't in themselves mean that the medlar wasn't native to the Eurasian countries listed, but only that the list may not be exhaustive.

A Little Greek and Roman History

The medlar was well known to the Greeks and the Romans, and it was also grown by the Assyrians and Babylonians. The Greeks had introduced the practice of grafting trees, which was originally a Chinese technique. In medlars, it enabled them to promote desirable characteristics and reduce less helpful ones such as their thorns, which remind me of those more dangerous ones on the blackthorn. Grafting facilitated easier cultivation and therefore land management, which in turn made for easier harvesting. The domestication of the medlar was underway.

Theophrastus of Eresus (c.371 to c.287 BCE), who is believed to have been a student of Plato's, was the author of two hugely important books on botany. His *Historia Plantarum* (which was translated as *Enquiry into Plants* by Sir Arthur Hort in 1916), suggests that he may have known the medlar, which he referred to as *sataneios*, describing it as a fragrant fruit, with an astringent taste.

The first century Greek physician, Pedanius Dioscorides, served as a surgeon in the Roman army and he also made time to write about trees. Two of them, *aronia* and *setanion*, described as astringent and slow to ripen, were named in his encyclopaedia of medicine *De materia medica*. Unfortunately, his description of *setanion* isn't quite definitive enough to support some views that this is the earliest written reference to a medlar.

Pliny the Elder's encyclopaedic account of the natural world, *Naturalis Historia*, contains several references to a fruit called *mespilis.* This fruit had a little calyx at the top and the tree could be propagated from a seed or a slip. His description doesn't add much to what Theophrastus has said, but he does give us a clue to the date of the fruit's introduction. Pliny asserted that if it was *mespilis* the tree didn't exist in Italy in Cato's time, from about 234 to 149 BCE. Some say that the Greeks brought it from Macedonia around the time of these wars (214 to 148 BCE) but the timing doesn't fit with the writing of *Naturalis Historia* unless the reference was to the fruit and not the tree. Others simply say that the medlar didn't arrive in Italy until the first century.

There is also a suggestion that Pliny's nephew, Pliny the Younger (c.61-c.112 CE), wrote about the use of the leaves, bark and roots of *mespili* to treat tumours. However, there is no mention of this in his correspondence, though a reference of this kind does appear in a book called *Medicina Plinii*, which is a fourth-century collection of medical recipes by an unknown author. This may be the source of the confusion.

A Continental Progress

We're now fairly sure that medlars had reached parts of northern Europe by the second century. Archaeobotanical finds across a wide area of the continent confirm the presence of seed debris dating back to between the first and third centuries in the canton of Thurgau in Switzerland, the Main-Kinzig district of Germany, locations in the Massif Central in the Aveyron department of southern France, Isere in south-eastern France, Brittany and urban environments in Annecy, Troyes, Reims and Lyon.

Véronique Zech-Matterne of the French National Centre for Scientific Research has written about medlars in a rural area at Novy-Chevrières in the Ardennes, dating from around the second or third century. She notes that before then, fruits were probably the privilege of the most affluent social classes, with the exception of wild berries, and that they spread into poorer parts of the countryside only slowly, unless they were native species. Corrie Bakels and Stefanie Jacomet's studies have led them to conclude that such luxury foods (in other words those which are not necessary for survival) may have been imported from the beginning of the Roman occupation, initially by the military, 'especially those of higher rank and/or those originating from the Mediterranean region', who wanted the kind of food they ate at home. Among the wider population, these fruits were probably adopted first in 'the households of Roman civilians and some privileged indigenous inhabitants'. This is because the 'towns in which they lived were often the locations where the food destined for the army was handled and traded'.

Medlars in Roman and Anglo-Saxon England

How did these undistinguished looking brown fruits with a descriptively crude nickname first make their way to England? The answer may lie with the Romans.

They had brought the long-standing Greek colony of Massalia, or Marseille, under their control in the first century, and they continued their progress north through France and east into south-western Germany, bringing their culture and habits with them. Some people think that the Romans had found the medlar growing in the south of France where the Greeks had originally introduced it. Others believe that medlars spread from Greece via the Roman Empire through northern Europe. One way or another, the fruit gradually made its way north-west.

Eventually the medlar found its way to England during the

Roman occupation. Although the fruit was present here, there is no evidence that medlar trees were cultivated or were found growing in England at this time.

Fortunately, and it is fortunate, the archaeological excavations undertaken at Silchester in Hampshire early in the twentieth century confirm the presence of medlars in England during the Roman era. The site in question was on a former Iron Age settlement which had been further developed by the new arrivals. Excavation work revealed the principal baths of the Roman town in a place formerly known as Insula XXIII, located near a brook and the town wall. Plant remains from the waterlogged contents of nearby wells and pits were clearly visible after passing them through wire sieves. In among these remains were 'stones of the medlar'. Just the two stones.

The discovery was written up soon afterwards in an article by William St John Hope and George E. Fox. They referred to the stones as coming from *Pyrus germanica*, a known synonym for *Mespilus germanica*. The stones were then examined by Clement Reid, a palaeobotanist and Fellow of the Royal Society, and he noted that the medlar, 'though cultivated by the Romans, was not previously known to have been introduced by them into England'. He described these two stones as hard and only about half the length of the cultivated fruit in his own collection. Reid had heard of a small medlar, only as large as a cherry, cultivated in Germany, and would have had stones of about the same size as those found at Silchester. This plausibly suggests that the Silchester medlars were a smaller variety than many modern cultivars.

This early twentieth century archaeological work, which is the only evidence we have of a Roman connection to the medlar in England, coincides with the start of the fruit's gradual and imperceptible slide from view as the twentieth century unfolded.

By the time archaeobotanist Dr Lisa Lodwick completed her own follow-up research into these early finds in 2002, the medlar was well and truly obscure in Britain, unknown and unrecognised.

Lodwick re-examined the plant remains and noted that these two stones of *Mespilus germanica* remained the only recorded finds of medlars from Roman England. Although there is no evidence of local cultivation, it can't be entirely ruled out. It is possible that the fruit might have been an exotic import for personal or community consumption, however there was nothing recorded then to suggest that medlar trees were intentionally grown by the Romans in England.

Although there is little written information about what happened to medlars during the centuries after the Roman Empire collapsed and the occupiers departed, the fruit doesn't seem to have disappeared altogether. Medlars played a medicinal and nutritional role in Anglo-Saxon life during this long period of our history stretching from the fifth to the eleventh century. We know that the relatively affluent Anglo-Saxon citizens of Southampton and London had access to a wide range of plant foods, including medlars, either grown here or imported from Europe. Any medlar cultivation, if only in gardens, private orchards and ecclesiastical settings, may have remained concentrated in the southern half of the country for a long time.

In 2012, Ruth Pelling, then the senior archaeobotanist at English Heritage, wrote an article for *Wessex Archaeology*. Her discussion about what people ate in the Anglo-Saxon period includes a list of plant foods which wouldn't look out of place in diets of the modern day:

The lack of detailed historical evidence for diet in the early and mid-Saxon period is such that we must rely on archaeological evidence for dietary reconstruction.

Evidence of the early Saxon diet remains scarce, although charred remains consistently include bread wheat, barley, with some oats and rye, occasional pulses and wild fruit and nuts.

By the mid-Saxon to late Saxon period the rise in urban environments such as Hamwic (Southampton), London, York and Winchester and associated build-up of urban waste has resulted in a comprehensive list of plant remains used in daily life. Field or broad beans, peas and cereal bran, consistently present in cess pits, were evidently prominent in the diet. A range of fruits (plum, sloe, apple, blackberry, raspberry, wild strawberry) and nuts (particularly hazelnut) and occasionally spices and flavourings such as mustard seeds, linseed or cultivated poppy, are recognised on both rural and urban sites.

The population of major mid-Saxon and late Saxon settlements such as Hamwic and London enjoyed a much more diverse diet including grape, fig, cumin, fennel, dill, coriander, watercress, lovage, cress, medlar fruit, mulberry, possibly lentils, quince and gooseberries as well as medicinal species including cannabis.

It is striking to see such a wide variety of foods, some of which would certainly have been cultivated here. Would other produce and fresh harvests possibly have returned with wool and cloth traders following their dealings across the Channel in Normandy and the Low Countries? Trading links with France may have been further strengthened after the marriage of Ethelred II to Emma of Normandy in the late tenth century.

Monastic physic gardens would have played an important role too, not only in helping to feed the population, but also by cultivating the kind of plants which could both relieve symptoms and possibly even cure ailments, a tradition and practice which continued for centuries.

Which brings us neatly to 'leechdoms', a term derived from the Old English *laecedom*, then Middle English *lechedom*, meaning 'medicine, medicament, healing'. One such leechdom contained in *Bald's Leechbook*, the manuscript of which is preserved in the British Library is an important reference. It may be dated on palaeological grounds to the middle of the tenth century. It relates a prescription for a swollen or distended stomach:

> [...] if the maw be swollen or distended; take some of the best wine, and green oil half so much, seethe the heads of wormwood therein and put this on nesh wool, smear therewith. Then give him the flesh to eat of little creatures, as of small fowls, sodden and roasted, and manifold kinds of apples, pears, medlars, peas moistened and sodden in vinegar and water, and in pretty sharp wine.

In 1912, Henry Wellcome, the American-born pharmaceutical entrepreneur who later became a British subject, wrote *Anglo-Saxon Leechcraft,* which he described as 'an historical sketch of early English medicine'. In it, he lists some of the native population's favoured fruits; including apples of various kinds, pears and medlars, which 'were known and appreciated'. Whether or not medlars were cultivated here in the Saxon era, medlars were available and they were being eaten.

We are not sure whether medlar trees were cultivated in England during the centuries immediately preceding or following the Norman Conquest in 1066. If the fruit wasn't growing here, it is possible that it was being brought over from France to satisfy the urban citizen in Southampton and London. Medlar trees can be very long-lived, two to three hundred years isn't unheard of, especially if they are planted in good ground. I'm immediately reminded of an astonishingly beautiful and productive example I know of in a private garden in Norfolk, which was planted in the early 1800s, and the medlar that George Herbert is believed to have planted in Somerset in 1632 reached an even greater age. Someone would have planted the medlar tree that bore the fruit that was harvested in 1266 at Westminster Abbey, but I expect that their identity will remain a mystery.

While relatively little was recorded about medlars in England at this time, there are records of medlars growing in France and Germany in the eighth and ninth centuries. It is possible that the fruit as well as the trees could have made their way across the English Channel from time to time, but we can't assume it. Historian John Harvey wrote in his book, *Medieval Gardens*, that even if medlars had been introduced here during the Roman era, as the Silchester finds suggest, they were still a rarity during those early centuries of the first milllenium. They may have been brought in occasionally by new arrivals from continental Europe, or they may have been regarded as a luxury food, effectively restricted to the higher echelons of Romano-British society.

Kathy L. Pearson's 1997 paper 'Nutrition and the Early-Medieval Diet' reviews the foods eaten by populations in the temperate land previously occupied by the Romans, including England. She describes the desirable plants to include in a well-stocked palace garden. On the list were the pome fruits: apples, pears, medlars and quinces. Some of them may have been pickled in vinegar or turned into wine. By now, there was a degree of sophistication in choosing strains of apple and pear, favouring ones that had good keeping qualities for example.

It is pleasing to know that the medlar didn't entirely disappear from view after the Romans left England. Elements of the diet of the Anglo-Saxons still seem familiar, and their practical interest in nutrition-based medicine may surprise the modern gardener and cook.

THE MIDDLE AGES

We stand on relatively firm ground in the thirteenth and fourteenth centuries, and there are clear and reliable documentary records of medlars growing in England, for example, at Westminster Abbey in the mid-thirteenth century. The abbey had several gardens, some within the walled precinct and others outside, each of which was run by a monk gardener, who was responsible for supplying the produce required by the abbey. In around 1266, Richard de Ware, the abbot of Westminster, directed the compilation of the abbey's 'customary', a register of its customs and practices. Among other things, it listed the fruits and vegetables to be provided for the Vigil of St Laurence, a highly venerated martyr, marked on 9 August. Medlars ('*mespila*') were specified, along with cherries in season, plums, pears and nuts.

Slightly later, in the royal household's account book for the fourteenth year of King Edward I's reign, 1285-86, a bill from Nicholas the Fruiterer refers to medlars among only a few types of fruit supplied, the others being pears, apples, quinces and nuts. The charge for all of these from Whitsuntide to November was £21 14s 1½d.

Other records, in this case from my old parish of Stepney in Tower Hamlets, to the east of the City of London, relate that a

Dominican friar, Henry Daniel, kept a garden there. John Harvey, the twentieth century authority on medieval plants and gardens, listed 252 varieties of plant grown by Daniel, which were described in his herbals as common, or sown and planted in gardens. These included the medlar.

Fourteenth-century botanist and physician, John Bray, notes that the medlar's 'beauty as a highly ornamental tree' accounts for the fact that it was reserved for the bishop in a partition of the palace orchard at Wells in Somerset in 1326. The relevant entry in the register book of Wells Cathedral recorded a grant of a piece of the garden to Canon Michael de Eston, and noted that 'a tree commonly called a medler growing in the said piece' near St Andrew's Well would remain in the bishop's hands. Medlar trees are still found in ecclesiastical settings, and there is at least one relatively youthful, productive medlar tree growing within the cathedral grounds at Wells.

Harvey commented that 'The work of the fourteenth-century herbalists, and especially the writings of Henry Daniel, bring us into the era of scientific certainties rather than guesswork.' A picture starts to emerge of the plants cultivated in England. Among those available to 'the typical medieval "herberur" working for a royal or noble patron' was the medlar tree, in leaf and flower in midsummer.

These records confirm that medlars had been established in England for about three hundred years by the time the English and French kings, Henry VIII and Francis I, feasted together in Calais.

The Eighteenth To The Twenty-First Century

As to the botanical naming of the medlar, it is from Carl Linnaeus' *Species plantarum* (1753) that we get our modern Latin name for it,

Mespilus germanica. When he came to replace long and complicated names for plants with a consistent scheme of binomials, Linnaeus called the medlar *Mespilus germanica*. This possibly came about because of a contemporary belief that it was native to Germany; medlars had certainly grown in this part of Europe for many centuries. Linnaeus' binomial system significantly predates the twentieth-century work done by Browicz, Vavilov, Evreinoff and Zukovski referred to earlier, to locate the medlar's original home, and now that we know about the ancient leaf impressions which were discovered at Burgtonna in the 1970s, it may be that the name is apt after all.

Victorian botanist, Leopold Hartley Grindon, noted that varieties of *Mespilus germanica* with 'enlarged and eatable fruit' were common in gardens in the south of England, and the produce was 'regularly brought to market'. It was certainly sold at the most famous of the British fruit and vegetable markets, Covent Garden. In a sketch 'Christmas (1851) in the Metropolis' published in 1853, we read about a 'tempting array of all that the depth of winter can produce', such as 'large English pineapples, pomegranates, brown biffins [apples] from Norfolk, and baskets of soft medlars'. Similarly, in Germany, the medlar was said to rank 'very high as a common fruit', and large quantities were 'disposed of on the market-stalls of all the principal cities'.

The literary historian and wine connoisseur George Saintsbury gave the medlar a ringing endorsement in his *Notes on a Cellar-Book*, first published in 1920. Addressing the question 'What, if anything, should be taken and eaten with after-dinner wine?' he remarked that as an accompaniment:

[…] the one fruit which seems to me to go best with *all* wine, from hock to sherry and from claret to port, is the medlar – an admirable and distinguished thing in and by itself, and a worthy mate for the best of liquors.

Sainstbury's enthusiasm for medlar fruit couldn't arrest its declining fortunes; the medlar's centuries-long popularity in England had been waning from around the end of the nineteenth century, and it took another downward turn in the aftermath of the First World War.

These days you might find them for sale in the mid to late autumn at an English market or greengrocer with local medlar contacts. A farmers' market might be an even better bet, but only in the season. There are several factors which influenced our subsiding interest in the medlar. It is true that a greater variety of affordable and imported fruit became available in the UK during the early years of the twentieth century. Another factor was consumer access to sugar at a more reasonable price than had previously been the case. These were undoubted challenges for the medlar, as was the alteration in our working patterns. More women were finding work outside the home and the eventual arrival of domestic refrigerators and freezers altered the daily rhythm of household provisioning. These socio-economic developments were significant and have continued.

Medlars need a little attention before they can be eaten as a fresh fruit or made into a tart, cake or curd. They couldn't compete with the appearance of novel, and more exotic, foods at a time when there was less time available for thoughtful preparation to bring out the best in them.

The medlar's golden age had long passed by the time Baird and Thieret wrote their respected article about the medlar for the journal *Economic Botany* in 1989. They described the fruit as 'neglected and forgotten', attributing its lack of popularity to, among other things, the necessity for bletting and its uninviting appearance when bletted.

Back to the Future in Farming

Agroforestry is a way of farming where agriculture includes the cultivation of trees as part of an integrated planting scheme. In practice, this means emphasising diversity of species to create vibrant, resilient and secure cropping communities.

Martin Crawford, the founding director of the Agroforestry Research Trust, established in 1992, co-authored *Food From Your Forest Garden* with Caroline Aitken in 2013. In their chapter on the medlar, they describe observed behaviour of the fruit in the West Country, where in warm summers the fruit can start to ripen, or blet, on the tree. I've seen this in Norfolk too, most recently in the warm early autumns of 2020 and 2022. They set out some of the medlar's nutritional benefits: vitamin A, phosphorus and potassium, and offer recipes for medlar and walnut slices as well as toffee medlars. It is lovely to see these creative ways of using the fruit.

Medlars earn their place in agroforestry planting schemes, which are an important component in regenerative farming systems. They are mid-sized trees, undemanding, tough, contributing additional layers of biodiversity in a mixed planting. On Devon's Dartington Estate you can see Crawford's model use of 'permanent shrub and tree cover to provide a self-sustaining food source' and several of the county's farmers are now putting this science into practice.

Suffolk has one of the longest established and most diverse agroforestry sites, Wakelyns Farm (www.wakelyns.co.uk). The Wakelyns Farm model is focused on shortening the food chain and increasing food security to provide the best produce and food within an organic system. Trees are cultivated in total of fifty-six alleys and lines all around the farm. Numbers 39-45 are a mixture of apple, pear, plum, quince, peach, apricot, medlar and other fruiting trees. Interplanted with other crops, medlar productivity benefits from all the natural below-the-soil line interactions achieved by using this approach. It is a way of farming that would have been familiar before the agricultural revolution in the late eighteenth century.

The Orchard Project (www.theorchardproject.org.uk) is committed to encouraging more diversity in 'top fruit' orchards. Examples include apple, pear, quince, medlar, plum: any fruit with stones or seeds surrounded by edible flesh growing on trees. Mixed planting of species boosts an orchard's overall productivity and eases the consequences of warmer winters which bring fewer chilling hours (a hindrance to productive cropping). The increased biodiversity helps mitigate the impact of pests and diseases though improved bio-resilience. Medlar, still a rare orchard tree in the UK, is on the Orchard Prjoect's list of candidate species to help achieve their objectives. This will help raise the medlar's profile and familiarise people with them.

The latest, and one of the most exciting, orchard and farming developments involving medlars is happening in Wales. Mat Feakins' family farm, on the edge of Abergavenny, Wales' food and drink capital, is now home to a newly laid out commercial orchard of medlars and cider apples. One hundred and twenty 'Nottingham' medlar trees were planted during the winter of 2021-2. A further two hundred will be settled in this coming winter, 2022-3, which will make it the UK's largest medlar orchard. They are planted on a south-facing slope. Although it will be a few years before the orchard produces a commercially viable quantity of fruit, Mr Feakins is taking a long view in terms of planning the venture. Forty acres of cider fruit have also been planted on standard stocks, with the aim of minimising the use of sprays and increasing the biodiversity on the farm. Mat says that 'traditionally, the fruit has mostly been turned into cheeses or jellies – some of our fruit will follow those paths but we are growing on a commercial basis for an alcoholic drink. It is important to keep these stories alive and to keep our historic traditions going. More people are sourcing locally grown and unique products'.

Permaculture in the Sky

When a leaking roof on their building sparked some urgent creative problem solving at Reading International Solidarity Centre (RISC) in 2001, the team decided to plant a permaculture forest garden in the sky. Permaculture is an approach to sustainable design that learns from nature. The roof garden is a huge success, not least the trio of heritage fruit trees which they planted, a medlar, a quince and a mulberry. This is especially impressive as all three grow in just 30 cm of soil. A generous crop of medlars is harvested every year. Seaweed fertilizer and wormery compost provide additional nutrients for the vast array of plants, shrubs and trees. This is probably one of the more unusual planting spots for a productive fruit tree, and I think it's worth including here, to encourage people to plant even where there may appear to be limited space or depth for roots to spread.

... And on the Ground

Dave Richards from RISC's Food4Families project, which has created over 25 food growing gardens in Reading over the past twelve years, spearheaded the permaculture project. He is a core member of the RISC team, which is working in partnership with the Royal Berkshire Hospital Trust to create a garden to complement its new Oasis Staff Health and Wellbeing Centre in Craven Road. This exciting project will create a haven just a stone's throw from the main entrance of the hospital, an opportunity to take time out, eat lunch and reconnect with nature, but also to give a new lease of life to a house and garden that are an important part of Reading's history. Dave has teamed up with experienced local landscaper, Chris Cox, of Mulberry Tree Landscapes, who created many award-winning RHS gardens for renowned designers such as Chris Beardshaw and Adam Frost.

The garden, which includes three medlar trees, will contribute to the hospital trust's net zero carbon green strategy: organic, water conserving, peat-free, using renewable, re-used or recycled materials for the hard landscaping where possible, and irrigating with harvested rainwater. Food waste from the Centre will be fed to wormeries to turn into concentrated plant food, and cardboard waste will be used as a weed-suppressing mulch. Increasing biodiversity will be a key element, with a pond, bug hotels, and bird and bat boxes installed around the site.

Medlars in Print

I hope I'm not imagining it, but the last decade has felt slightly more welcoming to the medlar. Are its fortunes really beginning to improve at long last? Prospect Books' decision to publish this book is one positive sign. Fruit tree nurseries tell me that they could sell more medlar trees to gardeners than are available each year. Yes, people do seem to be more interested in the medlar as a fruit and as an addition to the garden, albeit starting from a very low base. Another measure of interest is customer demand for medlar jelly, which I see throughout the year. The same has been true for the quince, which now attracts a wider following than it has had for several decades. They are more likely to turn up at the greengrocer, maybe as a surplus harvest kindly given by a nearby garden owner. I hope that we're approaching a tipping point for medlars.

Several of the current generation of British food writers have put medlar recipes into their books, possibly taking their inspiration from the late Jane Grigson who wrote so evocatively about them in her *Fruit Book*, first published in 2000. She acknowledges the fruit's medicinal qualities, referring to Dr Henri Leclerc's 1952 book, *La nèfle dans la thérapeutique d'antan* ('The Medlar in Ancient Medical Practice'). Leclerc wrote that medlar jelly was recommended by doctors in 1907, supported by a pre-war chemical analysis showing that its constituents made it a perfect remedy for various stomach complaints. Grigson recounts having spotted cartons of Italian medlars for sale at the smart Parisian grocers, Fauchon, on the Place de la Madeleine. Much larger than her own home-grown fruit, they were ripened and ready to eat, but slightly lacked the astringent finish of the best table medlars. I would have loved to introduce her to the sweet, citrussy 'Iranian' cultivar which blets on the tree.

She tells of the game of Ventura, traditionally played on St Martin's Eve, on account of which medlars were loved by children, as the basket of fruit was passed round the group and each of them eagerly hoped to select those fruits into which token coins had been tucked.

Mrs Grigson's recipe for medlar jelly has been joined by others in recent years: Nigel Slater's in his own fruit book, *Tender, Volume II* (2010), and Diana Henry included hers in *Salt, Sugar, Smoke* (2012). A few autumns ago, in her regular *Daily Telegraph* column, Xanthe Clay featured Mark Diacono's now legendary recipe for sticky medlar toffee pudding. The medlar's exposure to a new audience has definitely been helped by this coverage, as well as by social media activity. The old and forgotten is now being hailed as the latest trend in some quarters.

Eco-chef Tom Hunt, writing last harvest time in the *Guardian,* shared his recipe for medlar cheese. This is a set paste of slowly simmered medlar fruit pulp which perfectly complements blue cheese, and his recipe can be found online. I used to make little jars of medlar cheese, but as a solo fruit grower and preserve maker, I concluded that I would do better to focus on making medlar jelly. Judging by the number of jars of jelly sold each year, this product really resonates with individual consumers, as it pairs so well with all cheeses, game, charcuterie and meats other than beef. It is delicious with pork and lamb, and wonderful with venison.

Mark Diacono is well known to many of us as a keen grower, gardener and cook who has also written several award-winning books about his culinary and horticultural passions. He's lyrical about the more unusual vegetables, fruits and plants. His first thought when deciding what to grow is to remind himself about the fruit and vegetables he most likes to eat and which are tricky to get hold of and probably expensive to buy. His fruit choices usually start with his personal trio of 'unbuyables': the medlar, the mulberry and the quince. He planted around two dozen medlar trees at his former home on the banks of the River Otter in Devon. His superb recipe for medlar sticky toffee pudding is widely circulated each autumn on social media, and it is included here in the 'Medlars in the Kitchen' chapter with his and the publisher's kind permission.

Medlars in Europe: A Brief History

Across the English Channel, medlars were gaining prominence in the gardens of the grand estates and monasteries by the eighth century, both for the tree's ornamental beauty and the perceived nutritional value of the fruit. Charlemagne (747-814 CE) founded the Carolingian Empire in western and central

Europe. Towards the end of the eighth century, a text called the *Capitulare de villis* included instructions for the management of his estates. It directed that these gardens should contain a wide variety of plants, including medlars, known as *mespilarios* in Latin. The list of fruit trees included pear, plum, sorb, peach, quince, mulberry, fig and cherry. Another document, the *Brevium exempla,* issued by either Charlemagne or his son Louis the Pious, between about 800 and 817 CE, describes five crown estates in northern France where several properties included medlar trees in their mixed orchards of pear, apple, peach, hazel, walnut, mulberry and quince.

The 'Plan of St Gall', thought to originate from between 816 and 830 CE, has been described as 'a sophisticated architectural blueprint for a Utopian monastic community'. The document takes its name from the abbey where it has been kept since the twelfth century, when a monk folded it up to write about the life of St Martin. This may be how it came to be placed in the monastic library. Although the Benedictine monastery envisaged in the Plan was never built, it reveals much about medieval life. Drawn out on calfskin parchment in a monastery scriptorium at Reichenau, an island in Lake Constance, the detail extends from the basilica to the outbuildings and gardens. Unfolded, the calfskin parchment's significance was recognised in 1604. The Plan was first published that year by Henricus Canisius, primarily for the literary interest of its verses. Today, the Plan is held at the Stiftsbibliothek in St Gallen, under reference MS 1092. In 1979, Walter Horn and Ernest Born published a major study of the Plan. In volume two they described the cemetery, the grounds of which served also as an orchard. A verse couplet is inscribed on the Plan, at the location of a monumental cross. Horn and Born translated it as follows:

Among the trees of the soil, always the most sacred is the Cross
On which the fruits of eternal health are fragrant.

Fruit trees were to be planted in spaces between the burial plots. They included *mispolarius* (*Mespilus germanica*), alongside *sorbarius* (the service tree, *Sorbus domestica*). Horn and Born note that medieval monks contributed greatly to European horticulture by improving trees through selective breeding and grafting.

Moorish Spain was a centre of medlar cultivation by the twelfth century. John Harvey listed the plants grown in the south of the country in the Middle Ages by reference to five sources, two of which included the medlar: the *Book of Agriculture* by the Moorish agriculturist Ibn al-'Awwām, from around 1180, and the *Treatise of Agriculture* by Ibn Luyūn, a lawyer and ascetic, from 1348. Harvey also quoted John Claudius Loudon, who wrote in his nineteenth century *Encyclopaedia of Gardening* that the plants in Ibn al-'Awwām's list for the gardens of Seville were 'more numerous than those which were cultivated by the Greeks and Romans'. In Harvey's words, 'only some 76 of the 157 or so plants in Ibn al-'Awwām are found in Palladius' *Opus agriculturae*. But the medlar 'though well known in classical times, seems to have been relatively late in appearing in the southern garden flora'.

The medlar was well known and was highly regarded among cultivated fruits in Europe during the Middle Ages. In the early fourteenth century, Pietro de' Crescenzi, a retired lawyer and judge with an estate near Bologna in northern Italy, wrote a series of twelve books on agriculture and horticulture, known collectively as the *Liber ruralium commodorum*. The title loosely translates as 'the book of rural benefits'. In book eight, about pleasure gardens, de' Crescenzi described 'those things which enhance pleasure with respect to trees', such as planting fruit trees in harmonious rows and the making of marvellous and diverse grafts: 'many types of pear trees, apple trees, citrus trees, medlar trees, service trees, and the like can be grafted onto the same trunk'.

More than six hundred years later, excavation work at Ferrara, fifty kilometres from Bologna, revealed a brickwork pit, which had been used for a few years in the middle of the fifteenth century for the disposal of domestic rubbish from a middle or high-class urban household. A quarter of a million seeds were recovered, including pyrenes (fruit stones) of *Mespilus germanica*. They were evidence of a rich variety of fruit in the household. The authors of a 2005 paper on the Ferrara excavation described the medlar finds as quite abundant, noting that medlars were commonly recorded in 'archaeological sites in the region in the late Middle Ages'.

Medlars also feature in the late fourteenth-century text known as *Le Ménagier de Paris,* which was first published in the middle of the nineteenth century (and first translated into English in 1928 by Eileen Power under the title *The Goodman of Paris*). Anonymous and written by a bourgeois Parisian as a guide to running a household for his young wife, it was packed with advice on menu ideas for great lords and people of quality. Astonishingly, the first menu for a meat day consists of an eye-watering thirty-one dishes spread across six courses. Following the veal pasties, sausages, hare stew and roast rabbits, accompanied by other delicacies, the sixth and final course is of pears and comfits (a sweet consisting of a sugar-coated nut, seed, or other centre), medlars and peeled nuts, all washed down with a spiced wine, hippocras, and wafers. Another menu, comprising a modest twenty-four dishes, proposes a similar last course, but supplemented this time by sugar tarts and larded milk. For one of the suppers, medlars appear in the third course along with venison, dove and lark pasties, crayfish and herring.

Medlars in North America

Medlars are somewhat unfamiliar and hardly grown in North America, despite an amenable growing climate on the eastern seaboard, and in the wine growing areas of the West Coast.

A significant exception is at Scott Farm Orchard in Vermont (www.scottfarmvermont.com), a Landmark Trust USA Property. Here, they grow heritage apples as well as pears, quinces, persimmon and medlars, and supply fruit to a number of retail locations in the state, and a couple in New Hampshire and Massachusetts. They also distribute via wholesale partners, Myers Produce, Black River Produce, Food Connects, Marty's Local and others, all listed on their website.

In the middle of the twentieth century medlars were occasionally found in New York fruit stores, and possibly in other cities as well. But by the late 1980s the best-known produce dealers in New York were unacquainted with the fruit. The scarcity of the medlar is reflected by their omission in the Brooklyn Botanic Garden's *1200 Trees and Shrubs: Where to Buy Them,* issued in 1970. The 1987 edition of Andersen Horticultural Library's *Source List of Plants and Seeds*, which includes over 20,000 plants commercially available in North America, doesn't mention medlars either. Happily, the fruit is included in the Shakespeare collection at Brooklyn Botanic Garden.

The US National Arboretum in Washington D.C. (www.usna.usda.gov) has a solitary medlar tree. This singleton will be joined by three others, which are also 'Sultan' cultivars, in fall 2022 to create a Shakespeare Walk through the grounds, the four trees together representing the four plays in which they are mentioned: *As You Like It, Romeo and Juliet, Timon of Athens* and *Measure for Measure.* The current tree is well established and fruiting. Gerit Quealy, the author and editor of *Botanical Shakespeare*, is donating these new additions. The 'Sultan' cultivar is an abundant cropper, with fruits about two inches in diameter. With a fine flavour when bletted, they make good preserves.

It is difficult to pinpoint with any accuracy either the timing or method of the medlar's debut in North America. The earliest American horticultural works known to us that definitively include the medlar are Bernard McMahon's *The American Gardener's Calendar* of 1806, and William Cobbett's *The American Gardener* of 1819. Claims that it had been known around New Orleans at least two centuries ago are unverified. And it is unlikely that the trees would have survived for long in Florida, the south-eastern region being climactically unfavourable. At least three types of medlar, including the 'Nottingham', were reported as being 'tested' by the Louisiana State Experiment Station about 150 years ago. A report in 1899 on these so-called 'medlars' by the Louisiana Station is, in reality, on the loquat, *Eriobotrya japonica*, sometimes mistakenly called the Japanese medlar. Bearing in mind what we know about the optimum growing conditions for *Mespilus germanica* it would be very surprising if medlars had thrived in Louisiana.

The medlar is hardy as far north as Chicago, Lake Erie and Boston. The Morton Arboretum, just west of Chicago, has about twenty specimens, the oldest one dating back to 1937. The Arnold Arboretum, Jamaica Plain, Massachusetts, has some and they are considered to be perfectly hardy in central New York. In the West, medlars will thrive in coastal regions as far north as south-western British Columbia, and an occasional medlar tree may be seen in Vancouver as an espalier or as a specimen tree. I've noticed references to trees growing in the Nanoose Bay area on Vancouver Island and also Kootenay Lake in British Columbia.

By 1889 the medlar had been relatively widely planted in California. The California Nursery Company, near Oakland, claimed that the only medlar trees they knew were ornamental trees, obtained by people of Italian descent for their home orchard planting.

These days, the fruit is in demand from some other nationalities, Iranians for example, who made their home in the sunshine state in the late 1970s and early 1980s. Medlars, '*agzil*' in Farsi, are widely grown there and sold in the open on every street corner during the autumn. A friend, who spent part of her early childhood in Tehran, recalls her grandmother's admonishments when she helped herself to too many of these tempting sweet treats. In the traditional way, fruit, nuts and seeds would be placed in bowls on the table for everyone to help themselves as they passed by. The soft, ripe medlar's ability to ease constipation was well known, and a tummy could soon loosen itself if too many were feasted upon.

MEDLARS IN AUSTRALIA

It is most likely that medlars first made their way here with settlers from the UK. They grow especially well in the southern states of Tasmania and Victoria. Tasmania shares many of the climate characteristics of the temperate zones in the northern hemisphere. Near Launceston in the north of the island there is an independent brewery, Van Dieman Brewing, established on a family farm in 2009. The founder and brewer, Will Tatchell, was ahead of the craft beer curve on the island, and the world of hand-made, small batch beers was very much in its infancy.

We visited Will's farm in 2020, and he told us how he combines all his agricultural passion and the site's natural surroundings to create a broad range of beers and ales. There is a real sense of origin, time and place as well as people – the liquid summation of '*terroir*'. His mission is 'to brew excellent independent beer every day'. Read more about what he's doing and how he works at www.vandiemanbrewing.co.au. Needless to say, the farm hosts an established and very productive medlar tree. The medlar beer crafted by Will is unique in its style:

The medlar fruit provide this beer a bright stone fruit backbone with a subtle fruit-induced tartness. With a very low bitterness and minimal malt character, the acidity plays the lead role in keeping this fruited wild ale in balance. A little sweet and a little sour with equal parts fruity and fun; medlar is a beer as weird as its namesake fruit, stuck in a state of perpetual conflict – with rewarding results.

Will recommends pairing it with a fruit dessert and ice cream or a cheese platter for exceptional enjoyment. The abv is 7.5%. I've sampled it and everything he says about it is true. I wish I could buy his gorgeous beer in the UK.

Medlars in the Garden

Medlar trees are easy to grow, and I have listed the cultivars currently available in the UK, US and Australasia at the end of this chapter.

Select a sheltered, sunny spot with neutral to slightly acid soil for your chosen tree. Focus on supporting the invisible world below the soil line from the moment you plant it to help your tree thrive and fruit. If you create the conditions to hold moisture, support nutrients, fungi and worms to work together, your tree will flourish, giving you years of pleasure and a useful crop of fruit to boot. A single medlar, as it is self-fertile, will start cropping three years after settling into its home. Medlars are gracious and unusual additions to an orchard, admired for their fruit but also for their individual form and habit, requiring relatively little time and attention from the gardener's pruning shears. Its forgiving nature is one of the medlar's most attractive qualities.

I concentrate my medlar nurturing efforts in the autumn, after the harvest is gathered in, by distributing a layer of mulch around the base of each tree. I feed them with a cocktail of roughly equal parts of garden compost, home-made leaf mould, and partially rotted wood chip, all mixed together in a wheelbarrow for convenience. A couple of inches of this fragrant, rich, woody mixture, applied to damp or wet soil, locks in the available moisture and provides forage for worms and other creatures that live their hardworking lives on or just under the soil line.

I value the contribution made by our slithery teams of earthworms which create a network of tunnels down through which they pull the surface material to the medlars' feeder roots.

Having read Merlin Sheldrake's *The Entangled Life* (published in 2020, a few years after we'd planted our medlars), I now wish that I had included other fruit varieties or deciduous trees in a couple of the medlar orchard 'rooms'. In hindsight, this sounds like a counsel of perfection, but this is what is successfully practised in agroforestry, where a mixed planting of species strengthens the performance of each one. Biodiversity is really important when choosing what to grow, just as it is desirable for us when deciding what to eat. All is not lost, by any means, as we've established mixed native hedges of guelder rose, wayfaring tree, wild rose, spindle, dog rose, honeysuckle, blackthorn, dogwood, redcurrant and autumn raspberry alongside several of the medlar planting areas. These hedges provide essential habitat for nesting birds, shrews and hedgehogs. When it is time to work on the hedges, any cutting is done in layers, to enable the small debris to fall down through the branches, creating a natural mulch.

Sheldrake's book explains the essential role of fungi in sustaining life. Between them, fungi and roots create the vital micorrhizal underground web for transferring water, nitrogen, carbon and other essentials. It is far more than a way of communicating and information sharing, these webs act as a warning system and a powerful nutritional support network. The interdependence of coniferous and deciduous trees is facilitated by fungi: each of them calls for nutrition at different times of the growing year, thereby efficiently and effectively resourcing one another. Do read his book, it is fascinating.

Planting the medlar orchard 'rooms' has increased overall biodiversity at Eastgate. When we arrived in 2012 there were already hundreds of trees, including a dozen veteran Bramleys, a walnut growing up and over an ancient quince, oaks of varying vintages, beeches, a lime, a specimen tulip tree, maple trees of several kinds, cherry plum trees, alders, silver birches, several conifers, hornbeam, sweet and horse chestnut, rowan and ash. Many of the deciduous species were planted in the mid-1970s to form a shelter belt on two sides of our plot, which helpfully protects us from the worst of the prevailing winds. It has become a glorious woodland walk, rich with hibernation spots for hedgehogs, with spent wood piles that are gently rotting down, and a thriving understorey of successor field maples, cherry plums and blackthorn, among others.

This is the wider context in which the medlar orchard is set. Straightforward to grow, good to look at and long-lived, these trees thrive in temperate zones. The easy-going medlar provides year-round beauty and a productive harvest, and it is these qualities which sum up the medlar for me. They might attract you too. More than simply the years of pleasure and beauty a medlar tree brings, it will enhance the diversity in your garden and, if you eat the fruit in its natural state, it will also add unusual variety to your diet.

The branches, characteristically contorted, and double backing on themselves half Nelson style, are sufficiently structured in their winter bareness to support bird feeders, or to receive a garland of fairy lights, if you're so inclined. Medlar bark is a beautiful winter feature in its own right, as well as having some medicinal benefits when steeped in boiling water.

Garden owners plant fruit trees for all sorts of reasons, including harvest. In *The Book of Difficult Fruit*, author Kate Lebo describes how she feels about the medlar tree, despite being slightly less enthusiastic about the fruit itself:

The medlar tree itself has beautiful black curving boughs and soft white blossoms, the kind I have to hold myself back from joyfully crushing. At the end of the season, medlar fruits hang from the tree's bare branches like blackened Christmas ornaments.

Some Challenges, But Few Pests

By and large, the trees are easy to look after once they've been planted. Aside from the annual mulching and removing any dead, diseased (very rare) or internally crossing branches, they don't require regular pruning or lopping. Their eventual height is largely determined by the choice of rootstock, and they don't naturally grow much taller than five or six metres. If you want to control the height that is also fine, no harm will be done.

The climate is uppermost in my mind when I consider the challenges faced by all fruit trees, including medlars. In 2022, a summer of extreme heat followed hard on the heels of very little winter and spring rainfall in the eastern counties. This is the third such year since 2018 and I now plan for periods like this in Norfolk, which is the second driest county (after Essex) in the UK.

Although a few of the medlar trees sustained leaf scorch and some of the fruits were sunburnt, none gave up the ghost. The trees which were most severely affected, all of them 'Nottingham', were in three particular spots which I have recorded for future targeted help when this weather pattern recurs. One orchard 'room' which is planted with 22 six-year-old trees has behaved as if a perfectly 'normal' summer weather pattern prevailed. Whatever the reason for this, I'm grateful. Harvest and bletting will reveal the scale of any damage sustained by the sunburnt fruit. I'm crossing my fingers. The 'Nottingham' trees are all grafted onto *Crataegus* rootstock, and they've more than demonstrated their toughness and resilience. I hope that our assiduous annual mulching has helped too.

Muntjac deer can be a nuisance, especially for any very young trees. These muscular, diminutive deer, which are incidentally very good to eat, jump higher than you might expect. They easily breach our four-foot stock proof fences when they are in the mood. They love munching on young stems and trunks, and are capable of stripping away the bark all the way round – technically called ring-barking – which can kill if done to excess. Inexpensive plastic tree protectors successfully spared the trees in their early days. As the orchard matures, these hungry four-legged athletes are much less of a problem.

Other creatures pose different challenges. 'Starving' pigeons have a fondness for newly unfurled medlar leaves in the late winter. I find that bird-scaring tape is a cheap, low-tech and effective deterrent. I tie long lengths onto the branches in late February. It makes an impact, glinting menacingly in the light, and rattling impressively in a breeze. Too much leaf damage strains and stresses the trees, leading to reduced photosynthesis, which in turn impacts the yield. I've started leaving new growth long 'water shoots' on the trees. This may be unorthodox, and there is plenty of advice out there to say that these shoots are best removed, however I thought it worth experimenting. They are mostly high up and I am content to sacrifice a few leaves at that level in order to protect the established fruit bearing parts. It is pleasing to see a few disconsolate pigeons pecking at the moss on our lawn rather than watching them bounce their bulk along the branches of the trees, nibbling at fresh new leaf growth.

It is not just searing heat that challenges the orchard. Unseasonably cold spring weather has the power to petrify unopened flower buds. This was the story of 2021. Flowering was delayed by a month and pollinator activity was similarly affected. Honey bees can't operate in cold conditions, at temperatures lower than eight or nine degrees centigrade. If they are out on a cleansing flight and accidentally land, they can't muster the energy to take off again. Positive payback has been considerable, though, as the trees worked hard below the soil line and the crowns put on a lot of growth during the year. When harvest time came around the trees that had coped best were in a really sheltered spot, protected by a south or west facing wall. Nature makes sure I don't forget who's in charge. And I'm learning that there are compensations as long as I'm not impatient.

When harvest time approaches, I might spot ladybirds nestling in the deeper crevices at the calyx end of the rounder fruits. They are not problematic, but probably prefer to be liberated before the fruit is set aside for bletting. Our medlars have never been bothered by squirrels or wasps.

Speckled black webs with minute eggs, as yet unhatched into caterpillars, make an occasional appearance in the late summer. An affected area might be about eight inches by ten. They may be codling moth, which are not especially known for targeting medlar trees; apples, pears and quinces are their more frequent hosts. I might get three or four affected branches across the orchard each year, which I immediately remove with secateurs and burn.

GRAFTING

I defer to professional nurserymen in this highly skilled area of work. This is not my area of expertise, so I can't share success stories or failures. I understand from Karim Habibi at Keepers Nursery that the grafting timetable runs as follows:

Year One: Late winter, plant the rootstock. Summer, graft on the budwood/scion.

Year One/Two: Winter, top cut the growth.

Year Two: Summer, growing on.

Year Two/Three: Winter, one year old maiden ready to lift and transplant.

ROOTSTOCKS

Crataegus (hawthorn) rootstock is a great choice, highly compatible with medlar as well as being tough and resilient, however it can sucker energetically. Rootstock shoots will need to be removed from young and established trees. Like the medlar, *Crataegus* (hawthorn or white thorn) is a member of the *Rosaceae* family. It was originally native in Europe and western Asia (Eurasia) and has very successfully naturalised in the UK and similar temperate regions. Festooned with creamy white blossom, it is a signature feature in many hedgerows during May.

I wanted my orchard to grow to a maximum 'half-standard' height of about three or four metres and hawthorn does this. *Crataegus* has also helped to eliminate the thorniness of the wild medlar, unlike *Pyrus* (pear), which in turn can make a less durable graft despite its potential to produce a larger mature tree.

From a climate change point of view, hawthorn is pretty reliable under duress. The hot dry summers of recent years have tested the trees, and it is the rootstock that I most depend on to keep the trees alive. Hawthorn hasn't let me down yet.

Quince A, *Cydonia*, is the rootstock I've chosen for cultivars other than the 'Nottingham.' This has also performed well, although some suggest that it tolerates dry conditions less satisfactorily. Quince C is a successful dwarfing rootstock.

Practicalities and Planting

Medlars may be grown as standard, half-standard, or bush trees. The growers and nurseries listed on p. 179 are very helpful and will advise you on the options for your own plot. If you're nearby, it is well worth visiting The Newt at Bruton in Somerset. It was formerly known as Hapsden House, the home of Penelope Hobhouse, where you can admire a striking example of fan-trained medlar trees, interplanted with cherry, around the circular wall enclosing a main portion of the apple orchard.

Orchardists seem to fall into two groups, those who favour a well-formed canopy, perhaps conforming to an ideal of controlled beauty with the help of their pruning secateurs. I'm in the other group, and for me the medlar's gangly, awkward, almost tortuous double backing habit is a positively delightful sight. I adore these trees for their character and their resolute determination to do things their own way. Each of them is uniquely beautiful in my eyes, displaying a 'fantastic rusticity of its elbowed stems and branches'.

Medlars thrive when planted singly as they are self-fertile, hence you are spared the trouble of sourcing a suitable fertilization 'mate' as required by apples. In an orchard setting they mingle beautifully in a group, or accompanying their apple, pear and quince cousins. A sheltered, sunny spot in a well-drained, neutral to slightly acid soil is ideal.

Bare root, dormant young trees are supplied in time for planting during the winter quarter. At Eastgate, we dug square planting holes, to which we added leaf mould and garden compost, a handful of fish, blood and bone, and a few litres of water. The graft union should be set level with or slightly below the soil line. We staked and tied them into upright support posts with adjustable, flexible straps. Having back-filled the holes, each area was topped off with a water permeable square metre of grass and weed suppressant matting, which we secured with tent pegs. This was mostly removed a couple of years ago, once the roots were well down, and we embarked on the post-harvest round of compost, leaf mould and woodchip mulching to lock in existing moisture and to feed the soil. Keeping competition at bay and ensuring that there is no leaf stress during spells of hot weather is crucial during their first two or three years in the ground, and the trees will repay this care. The medlar kindergarten required several targeted, deep waterings during the dry summer of 2018, which was a four-hour workout for me each time I hauled my tailored hose around the plot. The same was necessary in 2020 especially for the very youngest trees.

If you have planted a 'maiden', a young grafted tree which resembles a whip, you have to help it 'crown up'. The first thing to do is reduce the planted height of the whip to about two metres. When the leaf buds start to appear in late winter, rub off all the buds below the level at which you'd like the crown to form. Wear thick, protective gloves to do this. Before long it will resemble a tree, probably enthusiastically pushing out some flowers which will need to be pinched out in the first year. The underground work of root formation is critical at this early stage and fruit bearing is a real distraction from root development for a juvenile medlar. Or any young fruit tree, come to that.

Our trees are now between five and fourteen years old and currently (2022) range in height from two to nearly four metres. The upper branches of the taller ones are easy to harvest from as I have an extendable fruit picker with a wire basket, affectionately referred to as 'the quidditch stick', which means I don't need to cart the Niwaki tripod ladder around as I move among the trees.

The medlar's early autumn palette is glorious, creating a richly coloured leafy background for the golden fruits as they plump up in readiness for picking. Late, if not the last of the fruit trees, they gradually start dropping their leaves in readiness to surrender their crop as autumn unfolds. This may not be everybody's favourite season, but for the medlar it really is the season of mellow fruitfulness, the foliage stunning us with endless variations on green, yellow, orange, russet and red. Sometimes it is possible to pick out all of these colours on a single leaf, individual spots of vibrancy building upon one another, reaching a crescendo of deep red, almost the colour of ox blood.

Harvesting and Bletting

Much of what I had learnt from reading about harvesting medlars, bletting and overnight frosts, has been challenged by my real-life, year-on-year experience looking after the orchard.

Apart from giving advice on medlar jelly, and sharing my experiences of making and setting, I'm often asked about harvesting and bletting. Most autumns I post a short film on Instagram and Facebook to help with aspects of harvest signals and the bletting process.

Medlars are climacteric fruits, which means they go on to ripen fully to an edible state – as apples, pears and quinces do – if they are harvested after they have completed their growth. The internet will tell you that the word 'blet' comes from the French verb, '*blettir*', and that this word means 'to make soft'. Norfolk-born botanist John Lindley coined the term in the second edition of his *Introduction to Botany*, published in 1835. He based it on a French word which described 'the peculiar bruised appearance' for which there was no English equivalent at the time. The French word '*blettir*' is still used for fruit, and has the same meaning as 'blet' in English: to arrive at an advanced stage of maturity. Lindley later refined his earlier scientific description of bletting as 'that kind of change which results in the formation of a brown colour, without putrefaction, as in the fruit of the medlar'. The softening is accompanied by an increase of soluble pectin, and a corresponding decrease of insoluble pectin. A material challenge for the preserve maker.

In Turkey, where medlars are both in the wild and in cultivation, there is a very old Turkish verb to describe bletting off the tree, '*göynümek*'. It more than hints at the medlar's ancient roots in Turkish culture.

Bletting starts on the inside of the fruit and works outwards. Mark Diacono describes it as 'a metaphor for rapidly fading beauty'. Incidentally, pears, melons, apricots, most stone fruits and avocados all do this, ideally in a warm kitchen. In the medlar's case, bletting works best in a naturally cool atmosphere.

There is a chapter on perry trees and their pears in Dan Saladino's *Eating to Extinction*. Perry pears resemble the medlar in terms of fruit size, about the size of a conker, their tendency to signal harvest readiness by falling to the ground in good numbers, and their capacity to blet. Perry pear trees may live for 250 years, as can medlar trees. If you bite into a perry pear a brief burst of sweetness is followed by bitter acids and astringent tannins. A ripe to pick medlar, if you can bite into it, lacks the pear's initial sweetness, but it has the same astringent tannic bitterness in spades. It makes me wonder whether medlars and perry pears are the closest of pome cousins.

I'm on the alert for harvest-ready cues and clues from the third week of October onwards. The date is the most obvious, and consequently easiest, cue to forget. Don't rush into harvesting before then. Beyond this, timing the harvest isn't a precise science. The signs include changing leaf colour, from dark green to yellow, orange, brown or red. You might notice that the fruit is starting to drop, just one or two to begin with, and any acceleration in the rate of fruit fall is a reliable sign. The majority of the autumnal leaves tend to remain on the trees during the harvest window, which lasts two or three weeks. There may also already be early signs of the softening and darkening of the fruit, which fully occurs during bletting. This is a sign to start picking. I find that night frosts and low temperatures are less reliable indicators than the internet and some books would have us believe. Not only this, twenty-first century autumns seem to be softer than the ones I remember from my youth.

Picking the fruit should only be done in dry weather. For speedy picking, the fruit should readily separate from its spur and it will helpfully still be hard and easy to handle. Rather like gathering golf balls. If you pick one and look carefully at the tiny stem, it shouldn't still be green in the middle. Harvesting medlars when they are already bletted, while appealing if you haven't got too much fruit to pick, is a frustratingly slow and precarious business if there are lots to gather in. When it is soft and edible, the medlar is more vulnerable to tearing where it is attached to the fruiting spur. It spoils quickly and it will either need to be eaten, processed, or frozen immediately if I've been hurried or careless in handling it. Unless you want to appreciate your medlars straight from the tree, one by one, it really is easier to catch them as they are ready to separate from the tree, still hard, but ripe for bletting. You can test their readiness by giving the trunk a firm shove or shaking a branch. If more than a handful of fruits cascade to the ground, go for it.

Picking up the windfalls, some of which may have already started bletting, is also part of the harvest. I always start by 'shaking the tree' and round up the fallen fruit which otherwise gets knocked off as I brush against the branches. Although it is popular with wildlife and beautiful to leave the grass longer, with Simon Greenwood's weekly help it is now kept short, as it saves lots of scrabbling around in damp grass for fallen fruit.

The harvested fruit should be placed somewhere cool and rodent-proof to blet, not in the refrigerator as the atmosphere is too dry. I pick the fruit straight into stackable, ventilated, plastic – and therefore reusable – mushroom or plum trays. This minimises handling the fruit. A tray like this will hold up to three kilos. If you ask your greengrocer, they will probably be happy to give you these free of charge. Any bletted fruits go straight into zip-lock bags for freezing, or into a separate tray if I need to make jelly immediately.

Place the fruit-filled trays in a cool garage, shed or outbuilding, if you have one, where they can complete the necessary final stage in naturally atmospheric conditions before they are ready to eat, freeze or use in a recipe. I use a north-east facing shed next to the house, and leave the door ajar. Please don't bring them into the house, unless you have a north facing and unheated room available. There is no need to dip the stalks in strong brine before bletting either.

Bletting is a process of transformation: the hard, pale, tannic flesh morphs into a mellow, sweet, dark, fragrant treat. If autumn has a flavour, I think the medlar has it in spades. Bringing them to a perfect, edible ripeness for the table, or to cook with, requires a natural atmosphere, time and patience. The fruit needs to be checked by hand every three to five days. In my early and inexperienced medlar life I examined them daily. Now I know better and can smell and see whether they need a review. Fingerless gloves are handy for this job. I've been known to run an extension lead from the house to power a light and if it is really cold, some heat. Download a good book or podcast to keep you company too.

The 'Westerveld' trees are the last to shed their leaves, and the fruit is the final one to be harvested, usually in December. Pick them too soon and they will dessicate, darken and harden rather than blet. Time and patience will be rewarded. Medlars hate to be rushed.

The branches don't stay bare for long in the winter; small, torpedo-shaped leaf buds are plainly visible by February. When it unfurls, the soft, new foliage is a bright green, occasionally with a red edged hue, and always tempting to touch when it fully opens in the second half of March. This is the first reveal of the new season. Perfectly round single flower buds are protected by their tapering sepals – the green parts of the calyx of a flower, enclosing the petals – as they plump up during their patient wait for their late spring debut. The leaves are broadly oblong. Lanceolate or tapering at each end, as foreshadowed by the leaf bud shapes, and varying in length depending on the cultivar, the leaves are between six and fifteen centimetres long and three to six centimetres wide.

The medlar's highly ornamental flowers start to appear in May, when they attract all kinds of pollinators, including honey bees. When pollinated, the hard, greenish fruitlets are visible from early June. The hermaphrodite flowers are similar on all the cultivars, usually between four and five centimetres in diameter. They appear singly on short spurs of one year old wood and older, clearly resembling many of their compatriots in the *Rosaceae* family. They have five elongated sepals which surround the five petals, which in turn encircle between thirty and forty stamens and an inferior five-carpelled, five-loculed ovary. Each carpel produces two ovules, only one of which develops into a seed.

It is difficult to distinguish between cultivars out of context, which may be a consequence of their relatively narrow genetic diversity as a species. This spring, I noticed that 'Macrocarpa' and 'Westerveld' have graceful, slightly tapered petals, and they rarely if ever break the five petal, single layer rule. The 'Nottingham' is a committed rule breaker, and it is not unusual to see a double layer of rounder petals.

Pink tinges seem to appear sometimes, but later in the flowering period. I'm not sure what drives this, and if you, the reader, know something about this, please let me know why you think it occurs. I'll continue to observe and maybe a consistent pattern will emerge.

The flowers finally open when the pollinator squad is out in force, which includes honey bees, which love the creamy white, often pink tinged, yellow centred blossoms. The opening is a gradual process, preceded by the slightest indications of what is to follow, delicate white peeping through cracks in the green. Medlar flowers are perfect landing pads for bees. As mentioned earlier, air temperatures are crucial because honey bees can't take off if it is too cold, below nine degrees centigrade. Some plants – oil seed rape is a relevant example as we're often surrounded by it – don't produce nectar unless it is comfortably double-digit centigrade outside. So much needs to align for pollination moments to occur. All I can do is create opportunities and cross my fingers.

Full medlar flowering, which can last between three and four weeks, also overlaps with the emergence of the leaves on our mulberry tree. For me this is the most reliable indicator that night frosts are probably behind us and that spring is well into its stride. This is one of the reasons cited for the usefulness of medlar trees and their cropping dependability. Medlar trees could only be improved for me if their distinctive five petalled, wild rose styled blossoms were scented.

SUMMER

The hard, young fruitlets are visible from the first weeks of June, already the bright green of the spring foliage is starting to darken slightly. Unpollinated and spent flowers dry to brown and by early July the successful, surviving ones are clearly identifiable. There may be some 'drop' as the season unfolds. The summer is the least dramatic of the medlar's four seasons. A few showers and bursts of warm sunshine are ideal company. If there are to be any codling moth sightings they appear in July or August. The fruit continues to grow for about five months until around the end of October.

Autumn

Autumn welcomes stunning burnished yellows, bronzes and reds to the leaves, which are untroubled by the arrival of cooler nights. Harvesting the fully grown, hard, tannic fruit begins. The final ripening, or bletting, happens off the tree. Bletting makes the hard fruits soft, darker, sweet and citrussy, ready to use in the kitchen.

Medlar trees are slow to lose their leaves, so choose a planting place which will offer you a vantage point from which to admire the autumn show. In my own orchard of 115 trees, each one proceeds towards and through autumn at its own pace. I think medlars look gorgeous planted singly, perhaps as a feature in the middle of a lawn, where you can admire them from all angles. The shelter of a south-west facing wall is another possibility, where they will fare better in cold spring weather. I know a trio of medlars near the east coast which flourish in a deep flower border. They form beautiful shrubs and wonderful half-standards, particularly when viewed from above, and they will also make a graceful contrast to a planting of beeches and limes, along lake margins and in company with weeping willows and silver birches.

Form and Structure

In the wild, a medlar grows as a thorny, shrubby bush. In their cultivated form, they mature into substantial, broad-in-the-beam specimens, wider than they are tall. The trunk, over time, may reach a foot in diameter. In favourable conditions they can grow at the rate of twelve inches in a year. Mature, grafted medlar trees are capable of reaching a height of four to six metres with the crown's breadth distinctively exceeding the tree's height. The older examples that I know here in Norfolk look to me as though they are reclining on the ground, with substantial layering branches helping to support the whole from a horizontal position. The oldest single example I have met appears to be made up of a series of individually layered trunks sprouting from several places. These are successfully integrated laterals, one of which might be the original trunk. This beautiful tree is believed to be a couple of hundred years old, and it is extraordinarily moving to stand among these lateral trunks during harvest, where I'm encircled by their strong arms as I admire the lichens and mosses that have made their home on this long-limbed ecosystem. The veteran tree continues to push out new growth, and in a good year it yields about 40 kg of fruit.

> [...] the medlar is a most distinct and handsome low-growing tree [...] about as distinct and pretty a tree as could well be desired.
> (A. D. Webster, 'The Medlar', *The Garden*, 9 November 1889)

> Everyone knows how picturesque an old medlar tree is [...] how beautiful it is in early summer when studded with its great white flowers amongst the large pale green foliage.
> (W. Goldring, 'Trees and Shrubs', *The Garden*, 21 July 1888)

These words encapsulate features which may have appealed to designer Julia Trevelyan Oman and her husband, Sir Roy Strong. They collected historic apple, quince and medlar trees and together they planted a medlar tunnel in the Laskett Gardens in Herefordshire, a county which Sir Roy, paraphrasing the Romantic poet John Keats, described as 'made for mists and mellow fruitfulness'.

Karim Habibi of Keepers Nursery in Kent says that a lot of his customers plant medlars for harvest, even in the smallest of gardens. Unsurprisingly, he sells out of medlars most years. He is the man to go to if you are keen to plant the 'Iranian' medlar, as this is the cultivar bred to enable the fruit to reliably blet on the branch.

Preferred Climate

Medlar trees thrive in temperate climates, zones five to eight, across the northern hemisphere. They also do well in the cooler regions of the southern hemisphere. There is a productive, but perhaps often overlooked, medlar tree in Wellington, New Zealand, at the Katherine Mansfield House and Garden. Leaning over the driveway, it sheds fruit every autumn. One of the volunteers harvests it to make medlar jelly which is sold in the visitors' shop there.

In Tasmania, a good friend of mine has successfully transplanted three medlar trees from his former plot in the fruit growing area of the Huon Valley. He's far from alone in growing medlars in Hobart. He met his first medlar thirty years ago in Ballarat, Victoria, and has loved them ever since.

One of the reasons medlars are tough and cope with fluctuations in temperature through the year is due to the choice of rootstock. As mentioned elsewhere, our 'Nottingham' trees are grafted onto hawthorn, which produces a half-standard tree, eventually about four metres in height. The other cultivars are happy on quince A, a semi-vigorous rootstock which also supports half-standard trees of a similar height.

Austria, Belgium, the Czech and Slovak republics, France, Germany, Netherlands, Romania, Spain, Switzerland, Balkans host them, and the foraging tradition which is much more deeply rooted on the continent of Europe continues to flourish. Medlars positively thrive in Turkey, where they grow on an almost commercial scale, producing thousands of tonnes of fruit to be harvested each autumn. I was once offered 1000 kg of Turkish medlars at a very fine price via Facebook. Some of the cultivars grown on the continent include 'Carya', 'Poland', 'Nottingham', 'Large Dutch', 'Suessmispel', 'Monstrueuse de Evreinoff', 'Delice de Vannes', and 'Apyrena' (a seedless variety).

CULTIVARS

The Royal Horticultural Society in the UK lists around twenty medlar cultivars by name. About half of these can be described as synonyms, including 'Elizabeth Garrett Anderson'. I'm still unsure whether, botanically, it is a 'Flanders Giant', a 'Royal', or a 'Nottingham'. It is frustrating and the best, albeit expensive, solution is to arrange for DNA testing.

This is the RHS reference list for *Mespilus germanica*. A reference for gardeners, it is relevant in determining eligible cultivars for National Collection holders:

'Nottingham' and 'Royal', two of the most readily available medlar cultivars.

'Flanders Giant' and 'Dutch' are also relatively easy to find. 'Bredase Reus', 'Macrocarpa', 'Breda' and 'Westerveld' can all be tracked down.

The 'Russian' appears to be available from one grower.

The 'Iranian' is exclusively bred and grafted by Keepers Nursery in Kent, originally by the company's founder, the late Hamid Habibi. It is the best cultivar by far as a table fruit, very closely followed by the 'Nottingham'.

A list of places where you may buy medlar trees can be found on p. 179. There is also a list for North America and Australasia.

What do we know about the cultivars that were available hundreds of years ago? In 1820, Henry Phillips, the horticultural authority, wrote that the 'Dutch' medlar, 'which is much larger and finer flavoured than the common sort, is the only kind now in request for planting in the garden or orchard'. By 1860, a wider range was available. There is a comprehensive list in Robert Hogg's *Fruit Manual*, which was published that year. The 'Dutch' was also known as the 'Broad-leaved Dutch', 'Gros Fruit', 'Gros Fruit Monstrueux', and 'Large Dutch'. Some of these synonyms have stuck. The 'Large Dutch' was still 'by far the [...] most generally grown of the cultivated medlars'. The fruit was also the largest, frequently two and a half inches in diameter. To my taste, it doesn't eat so well as a table fruit, but it is brilliant for preserves and beer making.

The 'Nottingham' (sometimes known as the 'Narrow-leaved Dutch', or 'Small Fruited') rarely exceeded an inch and half in diameter, but was 'more highly flavoured'. These days they are consistently around this size, sometimes close to two inches across. They are easily distinguished by the flat calyx, frequently with a pleasing and harmless fissure to one side. This is probably the best all-rounder. It eats very well as a fresh or table fruit, and definitely makes excellent preserves, beer and gin.

Hogg also referred to a third, the 'Stoneless', and to its alternative names of 'Sans Noyau' or 'Sans Pepins'. This was a similar shape to the 'Nottingham', but usually only three quarters of an inch in diameter. The flavour was inferior to the others, 'being less piquant'. The 'Royal' was introduced to England from France in 1860 by Thomas Rivers, who ran nurseries which had been established by his ancestor, John, at Sawbridgeworth in Hertfordshire.

I've already mentioned my favourite medlar, the 'Iranian'. It is sublime to eat one fresh from the tree. Juicy and sweet at the front of the mouth, followed by a finishing spritz of citrus, it is a highlight of the orchard in autumn. If any of them make it back to the house, I serve them with cheese and wine. They freeze perfectly, first on an open tray before packing them in a zip-lock bag. Defrost them on kitchen towel, or on a plate in the microwave, to eat as and when. This unique cultivar can be grafted on to two sorts of quince rootstock, 'quince C' for growing in a patio pot, or 'quince A' for planting as a half-standard in the ground. It offers those of us with a taste for the fresh fruit the opportunity to enjoy it straight from the branch. It is such a joy to savour the sweetness, juiciness and hint of citrus at the back of the mouth, a brilliant example of 'a date that tastes like it has sucked on a lemon'.

LIFESPAN OF A MEDLAR TREE

There is a lot of debate and a wide range of views about the potential longevity of *Mespilus germanica*, which the internet asserts may range from 30 to 150 years.

This is the story of the George Herbert medlar, which makes me positively reassess the long-term value of these trees. I would like to thank Peter Webster, webmaster of the George Herbert Facebook group, who generously and informatively responded to my email inquiry about the story of this very long-lived tree.

Herbert was a poet, and the rector of Bemerton near Salisbury from 1630-1633, and he planted a medlar tree in the rectory garden in 1632. Herbert's medlar was still living, although prostrate, in 1907, when it was skilfully regenerated by Thomas Sharpe, a county instructor in horticulture in Wiltshire. He'd been called in by Canon Warre to assist the tree. Sharpe 'inarched' a white thorn (hawthorn) onto a small shoot growing outwards from one of the decrepit trunks, which successfully imparted new life into the tree. By 1944 the tree had attained a girth of fifty-one inches at the point of inarchment, and the crown was twenty-eight feet in diameter. According to Professor Amy Charles, Herbert's biographer, writing in 1977, the medlar 'became a handsome, gnarled tree and flourished until 1973, when the roots were attacked by honey fungus'. What is unclear is whether this attack was fatal.

The rectory was sold into private hands in the 1980s, when we know that the garden was still home to two thriving medlar trees. The fruit had previously been available to pick each autumn. Today, there is a medlar growing in the same spot, however there are no records of a replacement having been planted. Looking at the 2012 photographs kindly sent to me by Mr Webster, it is hard to assess the likelihood of survival by the ancient tree. I hesitate to rule it out.

A supply of medlar fruit for the rector has now been successfully re-established: a medlar tree was planted in the grounds of the churchyard in 1993 to commemorate the 400th anniversary of the birth of George Herbert. The Church of England designates 27th February as his feast day and it is traditional, following the commemorative church service on the nearest Sunday, that the congregation is treated to medlar jelly made by the current rector. Even without Thomas Sharpe's timely intervention, it means the George Herbert medlar would have been alive for 275 years. As it is, it now seems to have achieved its 390th birthday.

Medlar Garden History: A Few Stories

Consistent with an increased interest in growing edibles during Elizabeth I's reign, there was a move to increase the range and variety of cultivated fruit and nuts by bringing otherwise unavailable types into England from Europe, especially from the plantsmen of the Low Countries. Literacy gradually increased throughout the population, and books about growing and cooking were being written, or translated, and then printed for publication in English during the sixteenth and seventeenth centuries.

A century earlier, medlars were held up in support of a questionable claim to the pre-eminence of England over France in its abundance and rich variety of fruit. Around 1549, a merchant named John Coke published *Debate Betwene the Heraldes*, a translation into English of the French tract *Le débat des hérauts d'armes de France et d'Angleterre*, which had been written anonymously about a hundred years earlier. A fictional account of a debate between the heralds of arms of England and France, the original text portrayed France as the superior nation, historically and culturally. Coke took the opportunity to adapt it for patriotic readers in England. In a caustic reply to a boast that the French had olives, almonds, figs and raisins, Coke's English herald said that even English children knew these were from Spain and not France. He went on to give examples of all manner of grains and fruits which England had in greater abundance than France, England being a 'fruitful and plenteous region'. Among these were medlars, as well as wardens, quinces, peaches, chestnuts 'and other delycious fruites servyng for all seasons of the yere'.

The Rhenish humanist Konrad Heresbach's book on husbandry *Rei rusticae libri quatuor* (1570) was translated from Latin into English by the poet Barnabe Googe, and published

in London in 1578 under the title *Four Books of Husbandrie, Gardening, Graff[t]ing, and Planting*. Heresbach had seen the medlar 'prosper very well' among oaks and woods in Germany. In order to keep the fruit, he advised, you should pick it before it was ripe, which I imagine meant when it was fully grown and before it was bletted and soft. Medlars were also preserved 'in sodden Wine, and Vinegar and Water'. It appears that in Heresbach's Germany, one type of tree with prickles grew widely in woods and thickets, producing fruit which was sour before it ripened, and which softened with the frost and winter cold. The other had no prickles and a large fruit. Heresbach attributed its development to diligent planting and grafting. It is hard to know how reliable an authority he was. The nineteenth-century writer on gardening George William Johnson described Heresbach's work as 'repleat with just observations' and superior to earlier books, but nevertheless imperfect: 'absurd practices, and superstitions the most gross, are given with all the earnestness of truth'. Johnson was particularly scathing about the surprising suggestion that the medlar could be grafted onto a pine tree, obviously a 'tissue of fables'. Nevertheless, his descriptions of the two types of medlar would be echoed a few years later in English herbals, for trees growing in England.

By this time, English writers were also expounding on techniques for planting and grafting. Born in Rivenhall, between Chelmsford and Colchester, farmer and poet Thomas Tusser lived at various times in Oxfordshire and London, at Eton College, at King's and Trinity Hall in Cambridge, and later in Suffolk, Norfolk, Essex and Cambridgeshire. In his 1573 work, *Five Hundred Points of Good Husbandry*, Tusser wrote for the month of January: 'Now set or remooue such stocks as ye looue'.

He went on to list medlars or 'marles' among the trees or fruit to be set or removed in that month. We haven't come across any other use of the name 'marle' for a medlar. *The Magazine of Botany & Gardening, British and Foreign* (1834) suggests that Tusser's word is *merles*, presumably from the French *merle*, which is translated as medlar in a seventeenth century dictionary.

Two years after the appearance of Tusser's *Five Hundred Points*, Leonard Mascall published a work with the full title *A Booke of the Arte and maner how to Plant and Graffe all sortes of trees, how to set Stones, and sowe Pepins, to make wylde trees to graffe on, as also remedies and medicines. With divers other newe practises, by one of the Abbey of Saint Vincent in Fraunce, practised with his owne handes, deuided into seven Chapters, as hereafter more playnely shall appeare, with an addition in the ende of this booke, of certayne Dutch practises, set forthe and Englished*. Mascall, clerk of the kitchen in the household of the Archbishop of Canterbury, used the words 'medler', 'medlar' and 'misple' interchangeably. He wrote that they were grafted on the 'white Hathorne tree' and the 'white thorne', both probably being references to the common hawthorn, the may tree. So grafted, the medlar would 'proue well, but yet small and sower fruite'. To graft one medlar on another, Mascall advised, was better:

> [S]ome men doe graffe first the wilding Cion [the wild scion], upon the Medlar stocke, and so when he is well taken and growne, then they graffe thereon the Medlar againe, the which doth make them more sweete, very great and faire.

In his *Herball* (1597), John Gerard confirmed that:

> being grafted in a white Thorn it prospereth wonderfull well, and bringeth forth fruit twise or thrise bigger than those that are not grafted at all, almost as great as little apples.

The whitethorn and the medlar were also paired by the

apothecary and herbalist John Parkinson in a 1629 work. He wrote that the medlar was known to thrive best on a white thorn.

In order that medlars, cherries and peaches would taste pleasant like spice and keep well, Mascall suggested that you should graft them on the 'franke Mulbery tree', wetting them in honey when doing so, and adding a little powder of some good spices, such as cloves, cinnamon or ginger. Grafting onto a mulberry or gooseberry (again using honey) would give you medlars two months before others, he asserted. Mascall firmly dismissed the suggestion by earlier writers that medlars without stones could be produced by grafting onto a quince. He described this as abuse and mockery, claiming that he had proved the contrary himself. In his view, to get medlars without stones, which would taste as sweet as honey, you should graft onto the 'Eglentine [Eglantine] or sweete Briar tree'.

According to Mrs. Evelyn Cecil, the inventor and writer Hugh Platt (1552-1608) wrote that the quince 'may well be grafted on a medlar', but not a medlar on a quince, something that had been 'proved by Master [Thomas] Hill'. Hill had published works on mathematics, physiology and astrology, and was the author of *The Profitable Arte of Gardening* (1563), a contender for the first book on gardening to be published in English. However, this isn't our experience, and the majority of our non-Nottingham cultivars are thriving on 'quince A' rootstock.

Diarist John Evelyn, who travelled extensively in Europe, married Mary, daughter of Sir Richard Browne, the king's ambassador to the French court. After their return to England in 1652, they lived for forty years at Sayes Court, by the Thames in Deptford, which was then still a village. The estate contained a three-storied Elizabethan mansion, of which Evelyn purchased the lease. His work *Directions for the Gardiner at Says-Court, But which may be of Use for Other Gardens*, was first transcribed and privately published in 1932. It contains a list of fruit trees in the garden in 1687. These include, planted in places not specifically described, medlars without stones. These appear to have belonged to a variety other than the 'Dutch' and the 'Neapolitan', because he refers to those separately from the 'One without Stones' in a 1664 catalogue of fruit trees, appended to his discourse *Silva*.

Under the heading 'Generall & Use-full Observations for the well-keeping of a GARDEN NURSERIE', Evelyn wrote:

> The very first thing a *Gardner* is to provide, is a *Nursery*, both for *Trees, plants & Flowers &c*, for which end, let there be an Aker of good ground divided into five parts, and well defended by pale or Wall […]
>
> Of these, let the largest part be for Fruit-trees, which should be divided into Beds for seedling stocks, and to remove the stocks into at farther distances in order to Graffing, and untill they be transplanted […]
>
> In the Fruite-tree Nursery These stocks are proper for the Severall kinds […]
>
> *Medlars*   One range of the white-thorne for Medlars.

Among 'Stocks Proper for GRAFTING each sort of Fruite-Trees' is the following:

> *Medlar* Graft on the White-thorne, or Quince stock neere the ground: it beares the second yeare.

A slightly modified version of this advice appears under the section 'TRYALS, IMPROVEMENTS & ORNAMENTS':

> Medlar: Graft a Medlar on the white-thorn or quince neere ye Earth it will beare the 2d or 3d yeare.

All of this is good and sound advice, which holds to this day. Later, in his *Kalendarium Hortense, or the Gard'ners Almanac*, Evelyn included medlars in a list of 'Fruits in Prime, or yet lasting' in November. A useful addition to the household.

In 1629, John Parkinson wrote *Paradisi in Sole Paradisus Terrestris*, prompting Charles I to bestow on him the title of Royal Botanist. Parkinson described three sorts of medlar, the greater and lesser English and the Neapolitan, though the last of these was probably a hawthorn, *Crataegus azarolus*, known as the azerole. The only differences between the greater and lesser English, he wrote, were the size of the fruit and the fact that the smaller type had pricks or thorns on the branches. He warned that the fruit was able to choke anyone who ate it before it had mellowed, but mellow medlars were eaten for their pleasant sweetness, and were sometimes served at the table as part of a dish of ripe fruit in season.

Three major herbals were published in England, between 1597 and 1653. The third and the most famous is Nicholas Culpeper's *The English Physitian* of 1652, now commonly known as *The Complete Herbal*. John Gerard's *Herball, or Generall Historie of Plantes* (1597), drew heavily on a 1583 work by the Flemish botanist Rembert Dodoens. Parkinson's herbal was his second major work, *Theatrum Botanicum: The Theater of Plantes, or An Herball of Large Extent*, of 1640.

Of these three, Culpeper was the most concise and arguably the most discriminating on the subject of the medlar, describing only two types, one of which had thorns and a smaller, less pleasant fruit than the other. This echoed Parkinson's distinction between the greater and the lesser, and descriptions of medlars in France by Jean Ruel in *De natura stirpium libri tres* (1536). Gerard and Parkinson went on to use the name more widely. Indeed, Parkinson's herbal presents the interesting challenge of trying to identify the various plants which he called medlars. In his discussion of these 'sundry sorts', he cited various botanists, including de l'Obel, Dodoens and Bauhin. The 'great manured medlar' (*Mespilus maxima sativa*) certainly sounds like a variety of *Mespilus germanica*: it was said to produce a fruit which contained five hard kernels and which was very harsh before it mellowed. The word 'great' seems to refer to the size of the tree rather than the fruit: it grew as large as a quince tree, but never so large as an apple. Parkinson suggested that it might have been Theophrastus' *sataneios*, Pliny's *setania* and Dioscorides' *epimelis* (also called *setanium*). He went on to contrast it with the 'ordinary or small medlar', which was ordinarily termed *Germanica*. These two types grew in many places 'here in our Land', but two others, the Italian and great white, had not yet been seen here.

Both he and Gerard wrote that the 'Medlar of Naples' was called 'Aronia'. Parkinson now identified this Neapolitan tree with the *anthedon* of Theoprastus and Pliny, and said it was grown only by 'a few lovers of rarities'.

He also described a dwarf medlar, a small woody shrub with reddish bark, which bore berries with little or no sap or juice, and the 'small bastard Medlar', whose dry berries were smaller than those of the hawthorn. As to the former, Gerard wrote of something similar, which grew in the Alps, the hills of Narbonne and the rocks of Mount Baldus near Verona, and which produced red fruit resembling haws.

Much earlier, in the late fourth or the early fifth century, Palladius Rutilius Taurus Aemilianus wrote an important agricultural work in fourteen books, known collectively as *Opus agriculturae* or *De re rustica*. Here we find clearly recognisable references to medlars as we now know them. Relatively little is known about Palladius, though he had referred in the text to having land in Italy and farms in Sardinia. He wrote on a huge range of topics, but there is a particular focus on fruit trees. In J.G. Fitch's modern translation, Palladius describes gathering and preserving the fruit before it has bletted:

> Medlars are gathered for keeping while not yet soft. They will last a long time on the tree, or in pitched jars or hung up in rows or (according to some) stored in vinegar-water [possibly a pickle?]. They should be gathered on a fine day at midday and buried in chaff, spaced out to prevent spoilage through contact with each other. Or they may be gathered half-ripe with their stalks, soaked in salt water for five days, and then dropped in sapa [a reduction of must, made by boiling] so as to swim in it. They are also kept in honey, but only if you collect them when very ripe.

In Book XIV, Palladius' poem on grafting describes how grafting a medlar on apple stock can be beneficial to the fruit. In an attempt to preserve the poetry of the original Latin, Thomas Owen offered this version in 1807:

> The medlar's entrails to be chang'd are form'd,
> They will with juice of snow-white hue abound

Professor Fitch's translation is clearer, if less gruesome:

> For her the medlar changes its stony flesh,
> expands and reddens, filled with snow-white juice.
> If the wild pear is used as grafting stock for a medlar:
> Supplanting the pear's hard fruit, scorned for its flavour,
> the medlar feels secure once its scion is installed:
> thus grafted, it grows even fiercer, doubly-armoured,
> and scares off greedy hands with its fearsome limbs.

Modern grafted medlar trees are, most advantageously, thornless.

In these extracts from Palladius' writings, *mespilis* fits the description of the medlar tree and the fruit, whatever Theophrastus and Pliny may have had in mind when they used the word. It seems reasonable to conclude that by the fifth century the Romans used *mespilis* to refer to what we now call *Mespilus germanica.*

Cassell's Popular Gardening, 1884, made no reference to the 'Royal', but said that the 'Dutch' was inferior in quality to the 'Common' ('Nottingham') for either jelly or dessert. The book recorded the practice and preferences of the time:

> Medlars thrive well in groups, or singly on lawns, or in orchards, or the fruit garden. The best form is a spreading bush resting on the turf, or neat standards from a yard to five feet high.

An 1810 survey in Worcestershire for the Board of Agriculture recommended that farmers should cultivate fruit. Light soils, it said, would produce medlars. They certainly do in Norfolk, on our very free draining light soil.

In two other early nineteenth-century surveys, in Gloucestershire, 1807, and in Staffordshire, 1813, there was discussion of the usefulness of the medlar in making hedges to enclose fields. One of the surveyors warned that, though medlars could be raised in great quantities by grafting onto whitethorn stems, it wasn't a good idea to put them in hedgerows, because people would be tempted to steal the fruit:

> The idle among the poor are already too prone to depredation, and would be still less inclined to work, if every hedge furnished the means of support.

The other writer was more sanguine, and perhaps more charitable. He recommended grafting crab with apple, plum with different kinds of plum, and whitethorn with medlar:

> Thus, will you have a very productive fruit-garden, without any waste of land, and a permanent fence, that will continue to the end of time [...] The all-bountiful Creator has supplied the earth with a vast variety of wholesome and nourishing fruits, and it is the duty of man to extend the blessings of Providence.

He went on to advise that, if your hedge produced too many plums and medlars for consumption in the neighbourhood:

> They would fatten hogs for pork, or the juice might be converted into spirit, which would probably be much superior to malt spirit, and perhaps little inferior to French brandy or rum.

I can vouch for pigs' fondness for medlars. I give the residual and unusable medlar pulp from my making to a local farmer's Saddleback pigs. Some also goes to a nearby couple who keep a few Norfolk Black pigs from time to time, for their own consumption.

Medlar Wood

Medlar wood is hard, fine-grained and flexible. It takes a good polish and is resistant to shock and abrasion. Examples of its uses include fine cabinet work, wheel spokes, inlaid work, canes and sticks, the latter being 'sometimes covered with numerous transverse gashes which is done in the stem during growth for the purposes of ornamentation', as J.R. Baird puts it.

We learn from a Dutch contributor to an Oxford Symposium in 1983 that medlar wood, being slow-growing and hard, was used in the Netherlands for making parts for windmills, 'especially some of the turning wheels'. Baird and Thieret (1989) found references to medlar in the production of charcoal, and as firewood which burns brightly and gives off good heat.

Way back, in the thirteenth century, we find the earliest surviving reference to magic in relation to the medlar tree. In book six of *De vegetabilibus*, Albertus Magnus wrote that enchanters sought out medlar wood to make fighters' staves, saying it had special strength for this purpose. The Basque *makila* (or *makhila*) has traditionally been made from living medlar wood. One Victorian travel writer called it a 'loaded medlar bludgeon'. It was carried for walking and for self-defence. The crafting of a *makila* in modern times is described in a Cadogan travel guide:

> Descended from the Basque shepherd's staff, they represent authority, justice and respect. The reliefs on the wood originate from incising the wild medlar in the forest, causing the sap to swerve around the cuts and form designs. The branch is cut in winter, peeled, stained with quicklime, and heat-straightened. The bottom is then fitted in brass or silver and hand-engraved with Basque motifs. The other end is topped with a horn grip and covered with plaited leather.

For more than two hundred years, *makhila* sticks have been handcrafted by seven generations of the Ainciart family, who live and work in the Basque village of Larressore, a short distance from Bayonne and Biarritz. The company became known as Ainciart Bergara in 1926, when Marie-Jeanne Ainciart married Jean Bergara.

Their son, granddaughter, and now great granddaughter, have continued the traditional and painstaking methods of growing, crafting and finishing their beautiful *makhila* sticks, and their work can be followed on Instagram. Liza Bergara recently published *Makhila,* the first full-length history of the subject, and hopefully the book will soon find an English translator.

Illustration for the néflier by the French botanical artist Pierre Turpin, taken from *Le Dictionnaire des sciences naturelles* (1816-1830).

Medieval anglers who wanted to make themselves a rod might have followed the advice of Juliana Berners. Born around 1388, Juliana was the prioress of the Priory of St Mary of Sopwell, Hertfordshire. She's believed to have written *The Boke of St Albans,* which included treatises on hawking, hunting, and fishing with an angle. The lower portion of her 'light and nimble' rod was to be made with a staff of hazel, willow or 'aspe' (aspen?), cut between Michaelmas and Candlemas. Once this had been heated in an oven, cooled, and dried for a month, it would be hollowed out and the top inserted. This would consist of a length of green hazel, attached to a 'fair shoot' of blackthorn, crab tree, medlar ('*medeler*') or *ienypre* (juniper?), cut in the same season as the staff.

Hertfordshire farmer William Ellis wrote in 1744: 'Of the Wood of the Wild Medlar we use to make Spokes for Wheels of Carts, and the Twigs of them serve for Carters Whips'.

Postscript: When is a Medlar a Loquat?

It is easy to confuse a novice. This is how I learnt the difference between a medlar and a loquat.

Medlars are close cousins of apples, pears and quinces, fleshy pome fruits with a central core containing seeds. It turns out that they are distant cousins twice removed of the loquat, which grows and fruits in warm subtropical summers. Loquats are often confused in translation with the medlar, as happened to me:

One spring, still in the first flush of love for my new medlar life, we visited very old friends in Marseille. We chatted about Eastgate Larder and the fruit I was working with, and there was great excitement when I told them that I had chosen to work with the medlar, *la nèfle*. To our surprise, they said the local *épicier* had *nèfles* for sale. I was mystified. It was June, six months adrift from medlar harvest time. More than anything, I was intrigued because retail sales of medlar fruit were pretty well unheard of, at least they were in the UK. Off we went to the shop on the corner of Boulevard Notre-Dame to buy some.

A beautiful display of what looked to me like smooth skinned apricots was advertised as *nèfles*. Quite unlike the medlars I was growing. Mystified, we bought some, returned to the apartment, where we proceeded to eat them. They are delicious, softly sweet with a cluster of glossy stones in the middle. It turned out that what we'd actually bought were Japanese loquats.

The confusion resides in a combination of language and eighteenth-century botanical science. Although *nèfle* (the fruit of the *néflier*), or *nispero, nespole, nespereira, nespola* in the countries encircling the Mediterranean, literally translates as medlar, the loquat is in fact *Eriobotrya japonica*, a very distant *Rosaceae* relative of the medlar that we're talking about here, *Mespilus germanica*. Late springtime in the northern hemisphere, there are beautiful Instagram photographs, hashtagged #medlar, each one of tempting loquats growing in sunny climes. Pretty well the only similarity between *Mespilus* and *Eriobotrya* is that they don't travel well when they are ripe, fragrant and ready to eat.

The confusion between the medlar and the loquat goes back a long way, to 1712, when a German physician and explorer, Englebert Kaempfer, published his *Amoenitatum Exoticarum*, including descriptions of plants he'd come across on his travels in Japan. By the way, and I didn't know this until recently, the loquat is a subtropical evergreen tree which is known to have been grown there as early as 1189 and which has been in Chinese cultivation for over 2000 years.

Athough Kaempfer described the loquat, it was the Swedish naturalist, Carl Peter Thunberg, who confusingly first called it

Mespilus. In his *Kaempferus Illustratus* he wrote up an 'explanation' of the plants which Kaempfer had found in Japan. Independently, Carl Linnaeus had ascribed the binomial *Mespilus germanica* to the medlar we're talking about in 1753. It is no wonder that confusion over loquats and medlars prevails.

Many of Thunberg's plant names later had to be revised. In 1822, John Lindley, the Norfolk born botanist who first accurately described the scientific and natural process of 'bletting', placed the loquat in a new genus, *Eriobotrya*. Despite the later botanical clarification, the loquat's linguistic association with the medlar has stuck. In France, the word *néflier* has simply replaced *bibassier*, the traditional French name for the loquat, among people growing and selling the fruit in the Midi.

Medlars in the Diet

When I embarked on my Eastgate Larder life in 2016-17, I was intent on getting the best out of my medlar fruit by making a consistent product that customers wanted to buy. I had a brief look at its chemical composition when I launched the spicy chutney in 2018, but since then I have discovered that there is much more to the medlar than its distinctive appearance.

The commissioning of this book has led me to dig deeper into the whole subject, including the fruit's dietary, nutritional and possible medicinal merit. There is a growing interest in almost 'forgotten' fruit species, notably on the continent of Europe, as a source of important compounds, with pharmacological and antimicrobial properties. This increase is due in part to a very real and pressing problem of a lack of diverse – as well as climate resistant – food resources. For growers, they have better pest and climate resistance than apples, pears, apricots, peaches and cherries. Medlars are still valued as a highly nutritional food in their original homelands, as much as they are respected for their anti-inflammatory and anti-bacterial properties, which have been appreciated and understood for centuries. Tisanes made with their leaves help staunch bleeding.

Writing authoritatively about the scientific composition of the medlar would have been more challenging, if not impossible, even a few years ago. There was relatively little peer-reviewed research available into the medlar, despite its long history both as a food source and in traditional and folk medicine. The World Health Organisation states that eighty percent of the world's population still uses traditional medicine to meet their primary healthcare needs. There are good reasons for this, in their opinion: medicinal plants are inexpensive relative to their pharmaceutical equivalents, and they produce fewer side effects. And they work. It should also be acknowledged that medicinal plants play an important role in new drug development.

The medlar's increased commercial importance as a fruit, as well as being regarded as a possible future 'nutraceutical', justifies the funding of more research into its chemical composition.

I've drawn on three academic research papers which were published in 2021. One of the research projects was undertaken in Turkey, where four to five thousand tonnes of medlars are harvested annually. Another was conducted in Poland, and the third in Romania. Medlars grow here too, and also support a longstanding foraging culture. The scientists who worked in this area have all used sophisticated processes to determine the composition of *Mespilus germanica*, which I won't detail here as they are comprehensively explained in the respective papers.

Turkish interest in wild fruits has increased in recent years and medlar fruit is widely enjoyed, both as a fresh seasonal fruit as well as in preserves, such as pickles made with hard medlars, which are often consumed as an appetizer in the winter months.

The Romanian scientists (C. Voaides *et al,* 2021) concluded:

Mespilus germanica represents a forgotten and abandoned species of fruit tree that is becoming more and more interesting and attractive due to the special properties of its fruits.

[… Its] fruits, leaves, bark and bud flowers revealed high

concentrations in antioxidant compounds (polyphenols and flavonoids), carotenoids, vitamins, minerals, etc. Highlighting the composition and properties of the medlar fruits is a very important aspect in order to rediscover this valuable fruit tree and to stimulate its cultivation and consumption.

Nutritional Composition

Research confirms that medlars contain measurable quantities of several minerals: magnesium, potassium (better than some other fruits), calcium, phosphorus and iron (immunity boosting).

Medlars are high in vitamin B, which supports a healthy nervous system. Vitamin C levels vary according to climate and methods of storage. They are impacted by cultivar, oxygen level in the air, light levels and temperatures. Although vitamin levels decline over time regardless of the context, Palliflex system storage can mitigate low levels of oxygen and carbon dioxide. (This is a pallet-based stacking system suitable for the long-term storage of soft fruits under various controlled atmosphere conditions.)

Medlars are relatively low in carbohydrate: fructose, glucose and sucrose, and dietary fibre. The sorbitol content, referred to in the Italian research paper, helps to sweeten and reduce the effect of the medlars' sugar (glucose and fructose content) on blood sugars, when compared to other sugars. They conclude that the overall sugar profile of medlars is lower than in apples and pears.

They are an important source of natural antioxidants, polyphenols, which play a protective role against inflammation, cancers, stroke and cardiovascular conditions. The polyphenol oxydase level in medlars is higher than for many other fruits (Akcay *et al.* 2016). Phenolic acids do two things: increase glucose uptake and the synthesis of glycogen. They also improve lipid profiles. They represent the largest proportion among the phenolic compounds identified in medlars. The levels of organic acids exceed the adult recommended daily requirement.

The Polish paper examined anti-oxidant and anti-diabetic activity of medlar fruit extract 'in vitro', and the findings indicated that they could have a role to play as part of a less expensive complementary strategy for management of type 2 diabetes, in combination with other nutritional and pharmacological strategies. Encouraging anti-diabetic results 'in vitro' need to be developed further 'in vivo'. Natural extracts of plant origin could be exploited as nutraceuticals and cost-effective food additives to support human and animal health.

The Turkish researchers, Cevahir and Bostan, also confirmed that medlar fruit may have a role to play in the development of nutraceuticals (Akbulet *et al.* 2016), with the potential to possibly play a dietary role in the management of type 2 diabetes.

Then and Now

Having looked at the science, I would like to briefly revisit the medlar's earliest 'known' appearance, and reflect on the possible reasons for humans noticing and experimenting with the fruit when they first encountered medlar bushes in the wild. Let's go back to the autumn of 1000 BCE, somewhere between the Caspian Sea and the Black Sea. As far as we know, they were low growing, thorny bushes covered in small, hard, golden-brownish fruits in the autumn. Cherry or olive sized, perhaps. They didn't signal that they were a danger in any of the ways that had been taught.

They are impenetrable. One, or a handful, end up slipped into a pouch or pocket, where they remain totally forgotten until a few days have passed. We're aware of a winey, fruity waft that we can't shake off. It is that oddball fruit that we'd seen a few days earlier, now soft and edible, sweet and nice tasting.

A hypothetical story, but nonetheless plausible. We've no

written records to help us to understand how humans discovered that the medlar was a useful and delicious fruit to forage in the cooler months. I can imagine that similar tales could be told about humans meeting early apples in Kazakhstan. It is hard to put ourselves in other people's shoes (for more than a few seconds), and it is just as hard to fully comprehend how our distant ancestors had to operate. They were schooled by family or group members in the ways of identifying 'new' edible plants, fruits and seeds, as safely as possible. These laid the foundations of a foraging tradition which continues to this day in many cultures.

At the same time, plant-based medicine was the only kind available, and it wouldn't be surprising that a process for testing, tasting and evaluating all possible uses of 'safe' new plant, seed, flower and fruit discoveries had grown up among the population. We have a great deal to thank them for. We are a cautiously inquisitive species, practised at evaluating new discoveries. This must be true, otherwise we would have died out. It is said that we've seen or tasted as many as six thousand plant types over the millennia that we've been around. In 1000 BCE there was still an enormous variety of vegetation growing in diverse geographies, compared to the much narrower range of each type that we grow and consume today.

This gradual reduction wasn't inevitable. In large part, it was due to the industrialised food system which came into being, imperceptibly to start with, about two hundred and fifty years ago, and which has taken off into the stratosphere since the end of the Second World War. Mechanisation and efficiency gains have powered economic growth and reduced employed headcount in every sector, including farming and food production. Supply has met global demand head on. It now feels to me as though we've overshot the sweet spot, that not so faraway place in lived memory where affordable, nutritious, naturally grown food was available and eaten more or less seasonally. One article I caught sight of suggests that the nutritional value of some everyday fruits and vegetables is now ten to fifteen percent of their prevailing values in the 1940s. Maybe this not so faraway place was familiar to my grannie's generation, born in the early 1900s. Wartime food rationing was aimed at preventing starvation within the poorer parts of our society, as well as limiting as far as possible a 'black market' in food and drink. Rationing was by no means perfect, but to its credit, few people were either malnourished or overweight when it finally ended in the early 1950s.

The late winter, early spring hunger gap of earlier centuries was real. I'm not trying to romanticise the past in any way, nor am I suggesting that a winter fruit like the medlar could singlehandedly ease the inevitable pangs. It did play its part, though, albeit a relatively minor one. The contemporary western diet, which has taken a firm hold in the UK during the last fifty years, has created a full-blown nutrition gap, which is gradually making us ill, and worse. Addictive, empty calories in the form of ultra-processed foods tempt us at every turn.

Despite this concerning picture, there are glimmers of hope. Seed stocks of old, currently uncultivated grains, rice and pulses, still exist, and companies like the award-winning Hodmedods (www.hodmedods.co.uk) are investing time, money and space in successfully trialling and growing on a range of crops in the UK's emerging regenerative farming sector.

I believe that the slight, but perceptible, uptick in interest in growing and eating medlar fruit goes hand in hand with encouraging and discernible shifts in our food and farming systems. The publication of the scientific research which I'm drawing on for this chapter is very timely. The Turkish scientists' interest in the medlar might be explained by their nation's significant production and consumption of the fresh, preserved and pickled fruit. Their modern cultivars include 'Bifera,' which is juicy and sweet, the 'Pospol', which is a little, long-fruited cultivar, 'Jumbo,' a large fruit, weighing as much as 65 g and the 'Uskudu', a new discovery.

The success of the 'slow food' movement, started in Italy in the 1980s, is now a global phenomenon. The UK's Agroforestry Research Trust, led by Martin Crawford, has significantly grown in influence since its early days in the 1990s. Regenerative farming is getting into its stride, creating long term and sustainable ways of producing quality food without the need for purchased inputs. Perennial herbal leys are grazed in rotation. These systems, if I can use this term, are intertwined in their thinking and approach, relentlessly focused on soil health and following the natural rhythms of the growing year. For farmers and growers, medlars are relatively pest free, and their climate resistance is greater than that of apples, pears, apricots, peaches and cherries.

Medlar trees have their place in agroforestry tree lines, as mentioned elsewhere. In East Anglia, they show up at Wakelyns in Suffolk, and on the Sandringham Estate, where organic principles were adopted several years ago. Slow Food UK recognises the threat to, and the value of, the medlar by including it in their Ark of Taste. The medlar orchard planted during the winter 2021-22 on a family farm near Abergavenny represents a conscious enriching of biodiversity in that beautiful place. It also illustrates what a possible commercial future might look like for this easy to grow fruit.

The other important piece to mention is the human gut, and the trillions of bacteria hosted by it, known collectively as the microbiome. Their secrets are gradually being revealed. The gut is described as our 'second brain', whose hosting role to the complex and important microbiome is crucial. Multiple aspects of our health and well-being are now more widely understood than at any time in our history. The best news is that we're now scientifically able to assess its health. It is possible to individualise results, so we can adjust the balance of our diet to better support it, our wider health and our well-being.

The medlar's role in human health remedies goes back a long way. Greek and Roman physicians considered that *mespilis* was a better medicine than food, due to its astringency, which gave it the binding qualities that are still valued today. This illustrates the value of the tannins and pectin in the fully grown, unbletted fruit. Simmered in water, medlars were a tried and tested solution for upset stomachs. They were used to relieve diarrhoea, which could be fatal if it were a prolonged attack. Even in the twentieth century, tannins were sought after as regulators of tummy trouble.

In his *Treatise on Fruit Trees* (1657) Ralph Austen alleged that medlar 'kernells bruised to dust and drunk in liquor' dissolved kidney stones, a most painful affliction. The suggested liquor was a mixture of wine and parsley root.

Other parts of the medlar, the leaves and bark, as well as the fruit may be used in medicinal preparations. Branch bark, boiled and orally administered helps to relieve fever. Bark and fruit can be used as a diuretic, and in pulp or syrup form it can help with enteritis. The fruit, on its own, helps with gut inflammation (served in milk, with the fruit's skin and seeds removed). It eases sore throats, soothes nerves, reduces bloating and menstrual irregularity.

As an aside, and I couldn't think where else to mention this, there is a centuries-long connection between the medlar and its power to ease menstrual discomfort of all kinds. Anecdotally, this is attributed to the appearance of the calyx end of the fruit. The latest scientific research is a more reliable route to attribution.

For more information, see the recent articles by G. Cevahir and S.-Z. Bostan, V. Cristofori, *et al*, C. Voaides *et al*, and A.K. Zolnierczyk *et al*, listed in the Bibliography.

Sourcing and Storing Medlars

October to December is the 'medlar quarter' across temperate zones of the northern hemisphere. If you're on the lookout for medlar fruit to pick, it becomes a bit easier to spot as it helpfully makes itself a little more visible on the trees, artistically contrasting with the dark green foliage. Early autumn rains add an eye-catching shine to the gradually fattening fruit, which takes on a golden hue. If you identify a tree that you'd like to harvest, subject to permission of course, then early October is a good time to find out who needs to be approached and ask them about picking the fruit when it's ready.

Equally, if you use a greengrocer or market where a few locally grown quinces turn up for sale in late September and early October, I would ask the grocer or stallholder whether they could either obtain some medlars for you, or make the necessary introduction so you could arrange to pick them when they are ready to harvest. It is not unusual to find that the owner of a quince tree may also have a medlar on their plot. The garden owner might be delighted to find a market for their fruit.

Climate change farmer and food writer Mark Diacono loves the fruity trio of mulberry, medlar and quince, rightly describing them as the 'delicious unbuyables'. They are his starting point when he's establishing a new planting of fruit trees, which is another possibility if you think the medlar is for you. The late summer fruiting mulberry and the autumnal medlar are largely invisible in a retail environment: they are highly seasonal and rarely, if ever, imported. Problematically for the shops, they are almost impossible to transport undamaged when they are ripe and ready to eat.

How wonderful it would be to look forward confidently to the medlar season coming round, anticipating baskets spilling over with medlars to choose from at the greengrocer or at a market stall in the run up to Christmas. Like the juicy high summer mulberry, bletted (ripe and flavoursome) medlars are extremely fragile. Half a dozen ready to eat 'Large Russian' fruit barely made it home undamaged on the one occasion I saw them temptingly displayed at a farmers' market. This physical vulnerability has contributed to the almost total lack of commercial-scale medlar orchards to supply ripe, ready-to-eat fruit to the wholesale market and onward to the retail customer.

For now, sourcing medlar fruit involves planting a tree of your own, having access to a tree in the garden of a friend or relative, or chatting up a medlar's 'guardian' in an accessible public setting, whether it might be your local park or a National Trust property. In this case, I suggest seeking out the head gardener and offering a donation in exchange for picked fruit. Rarely in my experience do the volunteer helpers want the fruit, so it's literally for the birds if it goes unused. In my early days sourcing fruit by this route, I always delivered a few jars of jelly and fruit cheese to the one in charge, who would share it with his or her team.

Our food system is dominated by supermarkets which handle more than seventy-five percent of the UK's food and grocery retail activity. They strive to deliver the physically perfect fresh produce that consumers have been encouraged to expect, thanks to advertising campaigns promoting visual perfection. The quirky medlar, the misshapen carrot, the plain and the unattractive fruit or vegetable are unwanted. They are cast aside. Medlars don't fit the modern retailing model and the twenty-first century, super streamlined supermarket supply chain would find it hard to accommodate them. So medlars, mulberries and quinces largely remain the domain of the gardener and the fortunate forager with access to a well planted community orchard or similar. The Brogdale National Fruit Collection in Kent has eight established and productive medlar trees (four cultivars), the fruit from which can amount to a few hundred kilos, and it sells out each autumn. I've read of Bristolian greengrocers occasionally having a basket or two of medlars for sale in the autumn, and it is said that they sell out pretty quickly too. I'm not sure whether these fruits are already bletted, or whether they are to be bletted at home.

Chefs obtain medlars from expert foragers. Norfolk based forager, Martin Denny, sources them from me as well as elsewhere, to supply several London restaurants. Modern British seasonal cooking has stimulated a healthy, in both senses, demand for all kinds of seasonal coastal and inland plants and fungi, as well as specially grown, hand-picked produce. I know of chefs who use medlar fruit from their own gardens. It is always a lovely surprise to see 'house' medlar jelly or fruit cheese on a menu.

As Jeremy Lee of Quo Vadis restaurant in London's Soho told me, not only is autumn his favourite season, the medlar is very near the top of his personal list of revered foods. It exactly fits the seasonal, unusual, flavoursome and versatile brief chefs look for and their customers appreciate. He makes medlar jelly, which is paired with feathered and furred game, on the side or in a jus. At home, I have one of Jeremy's beautifully illustrated and deliciously tempting autumn pudding menus from a few years ago, and in pride of place at the top of the bill, is the prune, medlar and almond tart. It was so good; served with cream, of course.

Occasionally, medlars may be spied at an autumn farmers' market or at an enterprising cheesemonger. If you see a basket of them, do treat yourself. And if you manage to lay your hands on more than you immediately require or can process, medlars will freeze very well. This way it is possible to keep a supply for use as a table fruit, or to make medlar juice for jelly and syrup, or as medlar pulp, throughout the year. A few of us do this, including the food historian and broadcaster, Dr Annie Gray.

Slow Food UK, the not-for-profit organisation which encourages better ways of eating, both locally and seasonally, has built an 'Ark of Taste', which is a collection of British foods which are in danger of being lost. The medlars grown by Andrew Tann at the family farm, Crapes Fruit Farm (www. crapes.wordpress.com) near Colchester in Essex, are on their list, and available to buy.

In Public and Private Gardens

Medlar trees hide in plain sight in public urban and rural spaces, National Trust gardens, community orchards, ecclesiastical settings, and sometimes in school grounds. At any rate, this is my experience in the UK. Medlar trees also turn up in private gardens – and more often than you might expect given how frequently people declare that this is a long forgotten and obscure fruit. Here in Norfolk, I found that once the word got round that I was interested in medlar fruit, the phone started ringing. Some garden owners can find the fruit irksome, and are only too happy to donate it for use elsewhere. When I started working with medlars and needed to supplement my own, help came in the shape of local National Trust properties, where head gardeners were happy to let me pick fruit in exchange for a donation to support their outdoor projects. This proved to be a successful model, replicated with private garden owners who rarely wanted payment for their dozens of kilos of medlars, but they all had a favourite charity to which I was delighted to contribute.

Birdcage Walk in London's St James's Park has a mature specimen which is propped with a yoke to support the canopy, and there is one in the Thames Embankment Gardens between the Savoy and the river. In West London, Blondin Park in Ealing has a mixed community orchard which includes medlar. They grow in the wilderness area at Hampton Court and in Dean's Yard, the site of the former monastery farmyard in Westminster, occasionally used by Westminster School.

In South East London there is a Medlar Street, formerly known as Orchard Row, with four established medlar trees planted along the street. The houses date back to 1870 when the orchard was removed. Every year people come along to pick the fruit, which they are free to do. Residents are enquiring at the council about replacing more recently planted species with medlars.

A productive medlar tree grows at Ham House, a National Trust property near the Thames. Volunteers gather the fruit to make medlar jelly for Christmas market sales. Medlars grow next to the Royal Shakespeare Company theatre in Stratford upon Avon and nearby in the garden of Anne Hathaway's former cottage home. Leicester Community Orchard has a medlar, as does Packwood's Memorial Orchard where you can sponsor a tree. In Sussex, in the garden of the seventeenth-century cottage, Monks House, bought by Leonard and

Virginia Woolf at Rodmell, a medlar tree grows. Christ Church, Oxford University, has a beautiful medlar tree, which is the subject of a long entry on their website, complete with recipes for medlar jelly.

Christopher Lloyd, the gardener creator of Great Dixter (his former home, and now a public garden), adored medlars as much for their aesthetic as for their distinctive essence in a jelly preserve. Kettle's Yard in Cambridge has a pair, one of which is planted outside the house, so that varying light levels cast distinct seasonal images depending on where you catch sight of it. Lincolnshire's Grimsthorpe Castle has six medlar trees. Midlands National Trust gardens at Brockhampton, Belton House, and Standen, all have medlar trees. You get the picture. Once you know what they look like, they seem to be everywhere.

The former picnic area adjacent to the regenerated walled garden at Blickling Hall, not far from our Norfolk home, has been undergoing a major restructure and is now incorporated into a mixed fruit and nut orchard. The lonely, established medlar tree has been joined by three additional 'Nottingham' trees which have been resited from my National Collection. They weren't doing well here, as I had crammed them too close to several long-established oaks. Blickling Hall has also received a young 'Bredase Reus', a 'Westerveld', an 'Iranian' and a 'Macrocarpa', which together will form a glade of eight trees alongside the new visitor centre. The wild flower underplanting extends across the whole area. This project is the brainchild of the dynamic new head gardener, Ed Atkinson, who has a plan to create an accessible and biodiverse orchard environment. It will engage and inspire the thousands of families and schoolchildren who visit Blickling each year, and the orchard's fruit will be made into preserves and chutneys to sell to visitors.

Cultivars Available in the UK

The Royal Horticultural Society in the UK lists around twenty medlar cultivars. About half of these are so called synonyms, including 'Elizabeth Garrett Anderson'. Botanically, I'm unsure whether it is a 'Flanders Giant', a 'Royal' or a 'Nottingham'. It is frustrating and the solution is to arrange DNA testing. One of the consequences of the medlar's gradual decline in popularity here in the last hundred or so years, is that a reduced number of trees generally will lead to fewer opportunities for the species to adapt to environmental change. Genetic diversity narrows as a result. A lack of economic interest results in habitat loss. We can play our own part in addressing this by planting a medlar of our own, and choosing a less commonly seen cultivar.

This is the *Mespilus germanica* reference list I had to work from when applying for Plant Heritage National Collection status:

— 'Breda', which produces a heavy crop of brownish red fruits. Pale flesh, juicy, slight satsuma on the nose, and a hint of cinnamon. Definitely moreish.

— 'Bredase Reus' is a good, late ripening sweet medlar. Caramel, little acidity. Originally from the Netherlands.

— 'Flanders Giant' produces good sized fruits for eating fresh or cooking with. Thicker texture, sweetness followed by a hint of sourness.

— 'Iranian' is a unique cultivar bred so the fruits ripen on the tree. They are very good for eating fresh. Darker flesh, very juicy, sweetness complemented by a definite citrus spritz at the back of the mouth.

— 'Large Dutch' is a very old, high-yielding and large-fruited variety with heavy, circular fruits. It is very vigorous and can

be recognised by its larger leaves. And the scale of the fruit. It is a good culinary cultivar, but has a less refined flavour and texture for eating fresh. Thicker texture, sweet, no caramel, reminds me most of medlar fruit cheese.

— 'Macrocarpa' has largish fruits. Less juicy and sweet. Reminds me of apple. Originally from the Netherlands.

— 'Nottingham' is the best-known and most readily available cultivar in the UK. It has good-tasting smaller/medium sized fruits, ideal for eating fresh at the table and for preserve making. It offers a pleasing balance of softness, juiciness, sweetness and hint of acidity to finish. It has a more upright habit than other cultivars. Holder of the Award of Garden Merit from the RHS.

— 'Royal' is a compact cultivar, producing somewhat rounder fruits. The fruits have a sweet creamy flesh and are good as a table fruit. Hint of pears, moderately juicy. A quality late ripening medlar, originally from the Netherlands.

— 'Large Russian' has very large fruits, somewhat flatter than the 'Large Dutch'. A somewhat drier texture than smaller cultivars. Ideal for preserve making rather than eating fresh.

— 'Westerveld' is one of the best later ripening medlars. Delicious eaten fresh and useful for preserves making. Sweetness with less acidity. Originally from the Netherlands.

The 'Common Dutch' is a smaller, round medlar which is worth mentioning because of its distinct and delicious notes of golden honeydew melon. We ate several to be absolutely sure we weren't imagining the flavour!

Will Sibley, past Master Fruiterer and leading authority on growing, has been working on a range of fruit trees for the home gardener. His 'Sibley's Patio Medlar' is grafted onto a dwarf rootstock, to thrive in a large pot, attaining a height of 1.2 metres. A four-year-old tree will produce a couple of dozen fruit to harvest between October and December.

Older Cultivars

What do we know about the medlar cultivars that were available hundreds of years ago?

Horticultural authority, Henry Phillips, wrote in 1820 that the 'Dutch' medlar, 'which is much larger and finer flavoured than the common sort, is the only kind now in request for planting in the garden or orchard'. By 1860, a wider range was available. There is a thorough list in Robert Hogg's *The Fruit Manual*, published in that year. The 'Dutch' was also known as the 'Broad-leaved Dutch', 'Gros Fruit', 'Gros Fruit Monstrueux', and 'Large Dutch'. Some of these synonyms have stuck and they add to the fun of trying to sort the synonyms from named cultivars.

The 'Dutch' was still by far the 'most generally grown of the cultivated medlars'. The fruit was also the largest, frequently two and a half inches in diameter. To my taste, it doesn't eat very well as a table fruit, but it is brilliant for preserves and beer making.

The 'Nottingham' (or 'Narrow-leaved Dutch' or 'Small Fruited') rarely exceeded an inch and half in diameter, but was 'more highly flavoured'. These days they are consistently around this size, and sometimes bigger. They are often distinguished by a flat calyx end, with a pleasing and harmless fissure on one side at this end.

Hogg also referred to a third, the 'Stoneless' (with its alternative names 'Sans Noyau' and 'Sans Pepins'. This was a similar shape to the Nottingham, but usually only three quarters of an inch in diameter. The flavour was 'inferior to that of the others, being less piquant'.

The 'Royal' was introduced to England from France in 1860

by Thomas Rivers, who ran nurseries which had been established by his ancestor, John Rivers, at Sawbridgeworth in Hertfordshire.

Cultivars Obtainable In America

'Breda Giant', 'Karadagskaya', 'Large Russian', 'Macrocarpa', 'Marron', 'Monstrueuse de Evreinoff', 'Nèfle de October', 'OSU 9-20', 'Pucia Super Mol', 'Royal', 'Sultan'.

Medlar Cultivars Available in Australasia

'Common medlar', 'Dutch', 'Nottingham'.

Storing Medlars in the Freezer

One of the attractions of the medlar to the pre-refrigeration generations was that the fully grown, hard fruit could have been kept in a cool place for a few weeks, unbletted, while tucked up in bran or straw. The gentle bletting process, bringing the fruit to its best for eating or cooking with, would extend the life of the fruit into the first weeks of January. Long storage of other fruit in their fresh form, apples and pears for example, wasn't always an option because of the varieties grown.

In the age of the domestic deep freeze, and this surprises many people, freezing is the most convenient way to hold the fruit at exactly the ripeness you're looking for.

If I'm keeping medlars to eat fresh I lay them in a single layer on greaseproof paper or baking parchment, before packing them into ziplock bags. On the day you want to eat them, remove what you need from the freezer and thaw the medlars slowly on a piece of kitchen towel. They will taste like newly bletted fruit. If you, your family and friends are cheese eaters at Christmas, a bowl of ripe medlars is an amusing addition to a cheese course. There may even be jokes about their looks.

Otherwise, bletted or a mixed bag of bletted and unbletted medlars for jelly making can be put straight into bags for immediate freezing. Like other frozen fruit, medlars will keep well for several months or longer.

If you're cooking with medlars it is possible to freeze strained medlar juice in spotlessly clean containers. I re-use plastic mineral water bottles for this, not quite full to the top to allow for expansion. Sieved medlar pulp can be frozen in quantities to suit your recipes. I don't detect any change in the quality of the end results from any of these steps.

Medlars in the Kitchen

'These fruits really come into their own when turned into a beautiful pinkish-red jelly to eat with cheese or game', says Raymond Blanc about the medlar. He's a devoted anglophile and has been the renowned chef patron of Belmond Le Manoir aux Quat'Saisons in Oxfordshire for more than thirty years. His book, *The Lost Orchard*, is packed with growing and tasting notes on many of the fruit varieties and cultivars he selected for his spectacular organic orchard in the hotel grounds at Great Milton. The orchard is filled with thousands of productive heritage fruit trees, including three medlars, which I believe he plans to increase. His French orchard in the eastern Franche-Comté region hosts three 'Dutch' medlar cultivars. As Blanc sadly reflects in his introduction, fifty-seven percent of Britain's traditional orchard areas have been lost in the last seventy years. In Oxfordshire alone, around ninety percent had been abandoned or destroyed. These are shocking numbers. Optimistically, he reminds us that 'even if you have a small garden, a backyard or a balcony, you can plant a heritage fruit tree. It is easy to train an apple, apricot or pear tree against a wall, or grow one in a container'. For example, the variety known as 'Sibley's Patio Medlar' is a tailor-made tree for a small space.

While the medlar may not be beautiful in the ways we've become used to, for example, glossy with the rosy glow of a Cox's Orange Pippin, it is a unique fruit which eats well 'au naturel' after gently bletting to perfumed ripeness. A dish of soft, fragrant, bletted medlars on the table is a talking point, a homegrown autumn and winter treat, which makes a fine partner for cheese and wine. While they add character and flavour to the table, they also add diversity to your gut. In early November, I love to eat newly picked 'Iranian' medlars, which have bletted on the tree. The juicy sweetness of the slightly grainy flesh is complemented by a spritz of citrus at the back of the mouth.

Blanc is not alone in his love of medlar jelly. Food writer Nigel Slater and chef Jeremy Lee are both fans of this glistening, delicate preserve which they make for themselves to serve with game or cheese. Medlar jelly can be flavoured in the jar if you want to add an extra dimension to something like baked gammon or a chicken. In a small bowl, fork together enough jelly and the spice you want to use. I use chilli flakes, or coarsely crushed peppercorns (white are good), ground cloves… whatever you want, really. Smear the mixture over your target and roast or bake in the usual way.

Medlar jelly makes a great partnership with pork, lamb, poultry, furred and feathered game, charcuterie and dairy cheeses. As a late autumn fruit, medlars do well in combination with partridge and pheasant. They complement the increasing range of quality savoury vegetarian and vegan foods which are available to buy. Medlars also make naturally sweet syrups, ice creams, cakes and tarts as well as alcoholic drinks. Their distinctive flavour loves citrus and spicy accents such as lemon, sweet and bitter orange, lime, star anise, pepper, chillies, cardamom, cloves or cinnamon. I focus on the delicate flavour of the medlar in the Eastgate Larder jelly that I make. It is made with three ingredients: the strained juice from simmering the fruit, lemon juice to boost the depressed pectin levels essential for a set, and sugar for keeping qualities. The addition of lemon enhances the natural citrus notes of the fruit.

Historically, medlars were usually, but not exclusively, eaten as a sweet table fruit in the winter months. In those countries where medlars are widely grown and can easily be bought as well as foraged in the wild, for example in Turkey, the fruit is often, but not always, consumed in its fresh form. Turkish pickled medlar recipes using the fully grown but unbletted fruit spring to mind. Medlars continue to thrive in this climate, just as they have done for hundreds, if not thousands, of years. The fruit is widely cultivated as larger and tastier fruit, as well as in its wild thorny form, in the hills and valleys of the north western region, around Samson, south of the Black Sea, and Canckkale and Bursa, which lie to the south of the Sea of Marmara. About four to five thousand tonnes are harvested each autumn, and they appear in the final weeks of the year in wholesale and retail markets across the country.

A few years ago, a Georgian family of five, newly arrived in the Midlands, bought a five-kilo box of fully grown medlars from my orchard to be bletted at their destination. The children's mother told me how much her young family was missing the taste of home and their autumn outings to forage for the fruit. I was so happy to send that box of fruit to her. We talked later about how she could locate a nearby medlar tree and obtain permission to collect the fruit, which I hope worked out.

On the face of it, there isn't much difference between the medlar cultivars to buy and grow in the UK. There are definitely those, usually the more compact cultivars, which are much better to eat fresh, and a couple of others which I would prefer not to eat as a table fruit. The biggest fruits I leave for preserves making and steeping in alcohol. The 'Iranian' medlar is so delicious to me that I never include this one in my preserves or gin making. Their exquisite sweetness on the tongue, followed up by a hint of citrus, is a total treat. The 'Nottingham' is a reliable all-rounder, for the table and preserve making. The largest of the cultivars, the 'Large Russian' and the 'Large Dutch' are easier to tackle with a small spoon but neither the texture or the flavour are rewarding. The local brewer I supply with fruit prefers a mix of cultivars.

Useful Equipment for Cooking with Medlars

When I started experimenting with medlars in the early days of my medlar relationship, I didn't have the right kit. Rather than rushing out to the shops to buy all the recommended pans and jelly stands I had read about, I compromised and made do with what I could find in my cupboards, which made the process seem like extremely hard work. In case this is a helpful aide memoire, here is the list of equipment I rely on every day that I'm cooking medlars:

Nine-litre preserving (maslin) pan or a large, wide-necked stainless-steel saucepan

Jelly bags and a stand (I bought mine from Lakeland. They've done hundreds of hours of service)

Soup ladle

Potato masher, long-handled

Coarse wire sieve (5 mm mesh is perfect)

Heatproof jug with a lip

Sturdy heatproof bowl

Long handled wooden spoon

Long handled silicon spatula (Kilner make good ones and are widely available)

Jam thermometer

Jam funnel for filling jars

Jars (these may be reused or recycled)

Lids (these must be new)
A supply of old, clean tea-towels

MEDLAR JELLY

The method for making medlar jelly is described here, and a recipe for the jelly can be found on p. 137. Recipes using medlar jelly start on p. 140.

Making medlar jelly is easy once you know how to deal with the low pectin level of bletted fruit. Prior to bletting, the fruit is impenetrably hard and astringently tannic. To recap, bletting is the post-harvest ripening phase that makes the fruit edible, and as it softens, darkens, and sweetens from the inside out, its pectin-rich flesh loses its pectin.

Adding home-made apple, crab-apple or, best of all, medlar pectin works nicely, but makes extra work. Preserving or jam sugar may be bought, as can bottles of liquid pectin such as Certo, and lemon juice is also effective. The easiest and least labour-intensive thing to do is to add a proportion of unbletted medlars to the preserving pan for the first boil. This is what I do, and I achieve the glistening soft set that I'm looking for much more often. Whenever I used preserving or jam sugar I ended up with a bouncy result, which I don't like to eat.

I make Eastgate Larder medlar jelly with ordinary granulated sugar, lemon juice and the strained juice from simmering the fruit: I start with roughly three-quarters of bletted to a quarter of unbletted medlars. To give you a rough idea of timings, I can make and jar a batch of jelly in about an hour, starting with one litre of juice in a three-litre capacity pan. The volume bubbles up when the mixture approaches setting point, so it is worth using a capacious pan. If I use the pressure cooker method for the first stage, the whole process takes about 90 minutes, from start to finish.

Medlar Juice: Two Methods

If you're making medlar jelly or syrup, making medlar juice is the first step, aiming to extract maximum flavour and colour from the medlars. There are two ways of doing this, either in an open pan or in a pressure cooker. The pressure cooker method is excellent for smaller quantities of fruit, it saves three-quarters of the simmering time of using the open pan method, and it makes a very well flavoured juice.

1. Open pan

You will need your largest and widest pan. Half fill the pan with bletted and rinsed medlars, fresh or previously frozen. Cover the fruit with water. The pan will be about three-quarters full.

Set the pan on the stove and bring it up to the boil, carefully mashing the fruit as it heats up. This increases the surface area of the fruit and boosts the final flavour. When it has reached boiling point, reduce the heat and simmer gently for an hour.

When the hour is up, take the pan off the heat and set aside.

2, Pressure Cooker

This works best in a 4.5 or 6 litre capacity pressure cooker. Pressure cooking the medlars yields about a litre of juice, enough to make 1 kg of jelly.

Put 900 g / 2 lbs of bletted, room temperature, squished or quartered medlars into the pressure cooker. Add 1 ½ litres / 50 fl oz of cold water. Clamp on the lid and put the pan on the stove. Bring it up to high pressure and keep it there for 10 minutes.

Take the pot off the heat and wait for the pressure to drop naturally, and the contents to stop bubbling, and then remove the lid.

Straining the Juice

You will need a jelly bag, its stand, a ladle and a wide-necked, heatproof, lipped jug.

Set up the jelly bag on its frame, making sure the elasticated neck of the bag is securely hooked onto the frame. Place the heatproof jug under the frame.

Carefully ladle the hot contents of the pan into the jelly bag taking care not to overfill it. You may need to repeat this step or set up another frame and bag if you have a lot of juice and fruit in the pan. Let the juice drip into the bowl or jug. This will take about an hour, or you can leave it overnight. A gentle squeeze at the end is fine, but too much manual interference will cloud the juice.

Measure the volume of medlar juice, which may be kept in the fridge until you're ready to use it for up to three days. It may also be stored in the freezer.

Medlar Pulp for Fruit Cheese and Other Things

If you want to bake with medlars, or make medlar cheese and chutney, the skins and stones need to be separated from the soft pulpy flesh.

If a recipe calls for a relatively small amount of pulp, let's say around 200 to 300 g (8 to 10 oz), it is possible to do this by hand with well bletted fruit. Assume you'll produce a roughly equal weight of pulp and debris, so start with just over twice the finished weight that you're after. Peel back the papery skin and discard. Then you need to sieve the remaining fruit to remove the five stones hidden in the pulpy mass. You do this by pushing the flesh through a large wire sieve into a bowl. Choose the largest sieve you can lay your hands on and set it over an equal sized bowl, steadied on a folded damp tea towel. The best sieve I've found has half centimetre holes and it fits neatly over a brown and cream Mason's mixing bowl. Using a soup ladle, I push a few hundred grams of the skinned fruit round and round, finally finishing with a cupped handful of medlar stones in the sieve and a fragrant puddle of medlar pulp in the bowl. In the early days of the business, a mouli was recommended for stone and pulp separation. It was useless. It is pretty sticky work with even a modest quantity. And frustratingly slow. My inner rule follower insisted I should do it once, which motivated me to find a better way. Here it is:

1. Open pan method

This produces a smooth medlar pulp. The resulting modest quantity of juice will only slightly taste of medlar due to the very brief cooking time, so you may or may not want to hang on to it. If you do, it'll refrigerate for three days or it can be frozen.

You will need your largest and widest pan. Put the bletted and rinsed fruit into your pan, and barely cover the medlars with water. Defrosted medlars may also be used. Bring the pan up to the boil and reduce the heat. Simmer for 15 minutes over gentle heat. While simmering, break down the fruit with a potato masher.

After 15 minutes turn off the heat, remove the pan from the stove and set aside to cool slightly. Set up a jelly bag on its frame, making sure the elasticated neck of the bag is hooked securely onto the frame. Place a heatproof bowl or jug under the frame. Carefully ladle the hot contents of the pan into the jelly bag. Wait a few minutes until the stream of juice flowing into the bowl or jug has slowed to a trickle.

Set up a coarse wire sieve over a sturdy bowl, which you've placed on a folded damp tea towel to keep it steady. Carefully unhook the bag of still warm medlars and invert the bag so the contents fall into the sieve. Depending on how much fruit you've simmered, this may need to be done in several stages.

Using either a ladle or a wooden spoon, push the pulpy mass around the sieve in a circular movement. You should soon notice smooth medlar pulp falling into the bowl below.

2. Pressure cooker method.

This time-saving way of simmering fruit is based on Catherine Phipps' excellent recipe for making quince cheese in *The Pressure Cooker Cookbook* (Ebury Press, 2012). I use a 4.5 litre WMF pressure cooker.

Put 900 g / 2 lbs of bletted, room temperature, squished or quartered medlars into the pressure cooker. Add 500 ml / 17 fl oz of cold water. Clamp on the lid and put the pan on the stove. Bring it up to high pressure and keep it there for 3 minutes. Remove the pot from the stove and let the pressure drop naturally. Patience is important, as the contents will still be bubbling vigorously.

When the pressure has completely dropped, undo and remove the lid. Carefully ladle the contents of the pan into a coarse sieve, set over a jug to catch the cooking liquid, which may be kept, or not.

When the fruity mass has stopped dripping, set the sieve over a sturdy bowl which you've placed on a folded damp tea towel to keep it steady. Using either a ladle or a wooden spoon, push the pulpy mass around the sieve in a circular movement. You should soon notice smooth medlar pulp falling into the bowl below. I scrape the underside of the sieve to remove pulp that's stuck.

The pulp can be kept in the fridge for up to three days if you're not using it immediately. It could also be stored in the freezer.

MEDLAR SYRUP

Medlar syrup is completely natural and gives you all the character of medlar in a concentrated form. It keeps brilliantly in the fridge and has no added sugar.

I use it in several ways at home, on yoghurt, over or swirled through ice cream, to improve a bowl of porridge, to add sweetness to pancakes, or possibly in the place of the caramel in an upside-down apple cake or in a tarte tatin.

When I'm roasting summer stone fruit or apples, pears and quinces, I drizzle the prepared fruit with a couple of spoonfuls of medlar syrup to replace all the sugar and half the butter.

The syrup came about as a result of my unsuccessful attempt to create medlar flavoured cider. Flavoured ciders are just that, apple cider blended with a flavoured syrup. Ideally, a contrasting flavour is added rather than a similar one. My stubbornness produced a perfectly nice but uninteresting drink. A waste of good cider.

Ingredients
1.2 litres / 2 pints of medlar juice

You need a wide, shallow pan to make this, and something good to listen to. Pour the medlar juice into your pan. Bring the pan up to boiling point and then reduce the heat to a gentle simmer. Watch over it, stirring occasionally, and skim off any gathering 'bubble scum'.

Gradually the juice thickens and reduces in volume. The colour will darken and the medlar flavour will intensify. Remove from the heat when the syrup has reached the desired consistency. Cool the syrup and pour it into a washed, rinsed and oven-dried screw-top jar. Store in the refrigerator so that it keeps for longer.

Beetroot Sandwich with Medlar Dressing

This sandwich was created by Sarah Pettegree. Her sandwich filling would be wonderful as a salad in its own right, scaled up to suit the numbers you're feeding.

Ingredients (makes two generous sandwiches)
1 medium cooked beetroot
30 g / 1 oz feta chopped
1 tbsp olive oil
2 tsp apple cider vinegar
1 tbsp medlar syrup
1 tbsp chopped mint
1 tbsp chia seeds
salt, to taste

Dice the beetroot and feta small, around ½ cm cubes. That way you'll keep more control of the contents and avoid beetroot lap and/or cleavage. Add the beetroot and feta to the other ingredients and mix.

This is ideal with a good sourdough. No need to butter the bread – just include enough of the syrup/oil dressing.

MUSTARD DRESSING

Medlar syrup is a useful ingredient in salad dressings; the one I make most often is a recipe for 'Mustard Dressing' from Catherine Phipps' first book on the subject, *The Pressure Cooker Cookbook*, which includes an essential teaspoonful of runny honey.

Eastgate's honey bees love foraging on oil seed rape, which is a favourite spring and early summer forage growing in the surrounding fields, producing a set honey. Medlar syrup is a good substitute for honey in dressings.

Ingredients
1 tbsp mustard (preferably Dijon)
1 tsp medlar syrup

1 clove of garlic, grated / shredded
2 tbsp cider vinegar
6 tbsp oil (I use a light olive oil. Groundnut and walnut are
  also very good)
salt and freshly ground pepper

Whisk the ingredients together and season with salt and pepper to taste. Add a little water if it needs thinning out. I make a double quantity of this dressing, pour it into a large jar and store it the larder.

Medlar Ripple Ice Cream

If I have a good quality shop bought (or better still, home-made) vanilla ice cream in the freezer, and some medlar syrup to hand, I'll make this. Dead easy to make and lovely eaten with a buttery lemon or orange shortbread biscuit on the side.

Ingredients
200 ml thick medlar syrup
1 litre vanilla ice cream, slightly softened

Soften the ice cream in the microwave at full power for 45 seconds. Alternatively, leave it out of the freezer for about 20 minutes. Swirl the medlar syrup through it, avoiding overmixing. Refreeze, and remove from the freezer 20 minutes before you want to serve it.

How Much Sugar?

Medlar jelly and medlar cheese recipes vary quite a lot when it comes to suggested quantities of sugar. It is important not to use so little that its essential preservative role is compromised. While the medlar is essentially a sweet fruit, the keeping qualities of the end product are extended if a fruit to sugar ratio of one-to-one is used. A longer shelf life is achieved by doing this, but it comes with a hefty hit of sweetness, which might not suit everyone.

I experimented before settling on the fruit and sugar proportions I've given here, which may be scaled up or down depending on how much jelly or fruit cheese you want to make:

For Jelly

1 litre / 35 fl oz medlar juice to 700 g / 1 ½ lbs granulated sugar.

For Cheese

1 kg / 2 ¼ lbs medlar pulp to 700 g / 1 ½ lbs granulated sugar.

The jelly and the cheese have a long shelf life and will keep well, unopened, in a cool cupboard for 18-24 months. Habitually, I refrigerate both after opening but this is not essential.

MEDLAR JELLY

I'm still taken by surprise at the medlar's transformation from a squishy brown fruit into a ruby coloured jelly of translucent beauty. This is true alchemy in a preserving pan. It brings out the best in game, adding a silkiness to pheasant, which can drily disappoint in the mouth, and it works well with pork and lamb. Beef demands something punchier: a fine Dijon mustard or eyewatering horseradish are my preferred accessories, so let's not go there with medlar. Top notch sausages, good quality charcuterie, savoury terrines and cheeses of every kind are welcoming to medlar jelly. It is gluten free, and suitable for vegetarians and vegans too. It adds a sweet liaison to sauces and braises if that's what you're after.

We're sentimental about medlar jelly in our house. My husband's much-loved nan used to make it for his grandad. It was a staple in his life, along with his teatime bread and cheese when he returned home from working on the farm.

This is how I make it:

Ingredients
1 litre / 35 fl oz medlar juice, made with three-quarters bletted
and a quarter unbletted medlars
700 g / 1 ½ lbs granulated sugar
50 ml / 2 fl oz pure lemon juice

Pour the medlar and lemon juices into a preserving pan or a large, wide saucepan. Put the pan on the stove and bring the juice up to boiling point. Weigh out the sugar, and add it to the pan. Stir with a long-handled spatula until it is dissolved.

Set up a jam thermometer by clipping it to the side of the pan, its bottom not quite touching the base of the pan. Bring the contents of the pan to boiling point. You want to maintain a rolling boil as you wait for the magical setting point to be reached. But not boiling so vigorously that the contents spill over.

Don't leave the pan unattended. If you must briefly leave the room, turn the temperature right down before you go. If I'm called to the phone, I sometimes forget my own advice, which gets messy.

Wash, rinse and oven dry your jars to sterilise them. I set the oven to 150°C / 300°F / gas mark 2 and place an oven tray of washed, drained and upright jars, not the lids, in there for 30 minutes, before turning off the heat. Leave the oven door closed.

This recipe makes enough for eight to ten 100 g / 4 oz jars. Try to find small jars if you can, as they look pretty on the table. They also make lovely presents and stocking fillers. Being small, they are less likely to lurk unfinished at the back of the fridge once they've been opened.

Testing for a Set and Filling the Jars

My aim is a scoopable, softly set and glistening medlar jelly. I don't want a stiff jelly that tastes overboiled and is chewy in the mouth.

This is what I do:

Setting point is near when your jam thermometer registers 104.5°C / 220°F in the pan. When this temperature is reached, carefully remove a dessert spoonful of the liquid jelly mixture from the pan and place it onto a pre-chilled saucer. Return the saucer to the fridge for a couple of minutes.

Remove your saucer from the fridge, and gently tilt it from side to side, as you look for any movement in the mixture. It is ready, when it is barely moving. Turn off the heat under your pan. If the jelly mixture is drifting across the saucer, I continue boiling the jelly mixture for another 3 to 5 minutes, before retesting.

To be absolutely certain that the setting point is reached, I double check by pushing my index finger across the surface of the jelly blob on the saucer, admiring the wrinkles that, hopefully, appear.

When you judge that the mixture is ready to pot up, remove the pan from the heat. Bring the sterilised jars to where you are going to fill them. Decant the contents of the pan into a spotlessly clean, lipped pouring jug.

Let the contents stand for a couple of minutes to allow the unavoidable 'bubble scum' to settle on the surface. I use a round bladed knife to ease this layer away from the lip of the jug at the same time as I carefully fill my jars. Pour any leftover mixture into a ramekin. This is so that I can check the end result when it is cold and set, without opening one of my precious jars.

Screw on the lids and briefly invert the filled jars to sterilise the lids' interior surface. When they are tepid, give the lids another twist to tighten them off. Label and date the jars. Admire their beautiful colour. Store in a cool, dark place.

RECIPES USING MEDLAR JELLY

Pheasant Breasts with Thyme

This is a recipe I wrote for a crowdfunded project, *The Norfolk Cook Book*. It is an easy autumn supper for four people. Pheasant can be dry and rather dull; this is my attempt at improving it. I serve it with plenty of leafy greens and roasted root vegetables, whatever I have to hand. Beetroot dressed with a dash of red wine vinegar or medlar vinegar is good, as are roasted parsnips and carrots.

Ingredients
4 plump pheasant breasts
1 red onion, finely sliced
5 whole sprigs thyme
1 unpeeled russet apple, sliced into half moons
2 tbsp / 30 ml / 1 ½ fl oz medlar jelly
olive oil and butter
100 ml / 3 ½ fl oz dry sherry
salt and pepper to taste

Melt a knob of butter and half a tablespoon of olive oil in a heavy, shallow pan. Add the sliced onion and thyme sprigs, and fry gently until the onion is starting to caramelise around the edges. This will take a few minutes. Remove the onions to a plate and set aside.

Add a little more butter to the pan, and when it is foaming, add the apple slices and turn them carefully until they are well coloured. Add the browned apple slices to the onions.

Season the pheasant breasts with sea salt and ground black pepper. Add a little more oil and butter to the pan if needed, and brown the seasoned pheasant breasts on both sides, over a medium heat. Cook them for a further 3 minutes. You want them to be as tender as possible.

Pour in the sherry, let it bubble, and deglaze the pan. Add the medlar jelly, and increase the heat for a couple of minutes to melt the jelly. If the pan feels crowded, lift the pheasant onto the plate with the onion and apple slices while you complete this step. Return the onions and apple (and pheasant) to the pan.

Bring the pan up to a simmer and serve immediately.

VENISON SAUSAGES WITH ONION GRAVY

Venison works really well with fruity accompaniments, and we're fortunate that our local butcher makes excellent sausages with this wild, seasonally available meat. Serve with buttery mash or baked potatoes and lots of green veg.

Ingredients (serves four)
2-3 venison sausages per person, depending on appetite
2 large red or white onions, finely sliced
olive oil and a knob of butter
1 heaped tbsp plain flour
1 litre / 35 fl oz hot game or vegetable stock
thyme, a few sprigs or a large pinch of good quality dried thyme
medlar jelly to taste
salt and ground black pepper

Preheat the oven to 180°C / 160°C fan / 350°F / gas mark 4. You'll need a large baking sheet, covered with baking parchment and a wide, heavy, shallow pan (Le Creuset is ideal).

Melt the oil and butter into a heavy, wide, shallow pan and add the onions and thyme. Stir to coat them evenly with the butter and oil. Increase the heat so they gradually start to cook – we're aiming for a soft, glistening mound of sweet, fragrant onions, with no hint of crispiness or fried edges. This will take about 20 minutes. You may want, or need, to add a little more butter. Partially cover the pan with a lid.

When the onions are soft and collapsed, it is time to put the sausages onto a baking sheet and into the oven. They will need to be turned over at half time, so set the timer for 15 minutes.

Now that the onions are soft and glistening, add a tablespoonful of plain flour and mix in thoroughly with a wooden spoon. Cook this onion roux gently without browning it for 2 minutes. Add the hot stock, one ladle at a time. Incorporate the liquid completely after each addition to reduce the chance of lumpiness.

Bring the sauce to a gentle simmer, and stir in the medlar jelly until it has melted. Check the sausages when the timer buzzes, turn them over and return them to the oven. Reset the timer for 10 minutes.

Check the seasoning of the onion gravy – depending on your stock, you may need more salt. A generous grinding of black pepper should be added now. Check seasoning again, make sure it is piping hot, and serve.

Pan-Fried Scallops with Apple, Medlar Jelly and Truffle

Scallops work brilliantly with medlar jelly. I confess that I had not considered trying this pairing until I came across the original recipe, using crab apple jelly, in Stuart Ovenden's *The Orchard Cook*. It's a genius combination. Thank you, Stuart for allowing me to reproduce it here.

Ingredients (serves 12 as a hot canape, or 4 as a starter)
4 tsp medlar jelly
1 eating apple
juice of 1 lemon
12 fresh hand dived scallops, roe on or off, as you prefer.
1 summer truffle

If serving as a starter:
watercress
crusty bread

Core the apple, then use a mandolin to cut into approximately 3 mm slices. Use a knife to cut into matchsticks, then transfer to a small bowl. Squeeze over the juice of half of the lemon. Set to one side.

Pat the scallops dry with kitchen paper and season with salt and pepper. Heat a heavy-bottomed frying pan, then add a splash of olive oil. When the oil is hot, add the scallops one-by-one. Think of the pan as a clock face; start at 12 and place clockwise in a circle (if they're spaced evenly, the final scallop should land at about 11).

After 2 minutes start flipping the scallops – start at 12 as before. This process helps you keep track of when each one went in to keep an even cooking time; leave them on the heat for a further minute.

Take off the heat and squeeze over the juice from the other half of lemon. Serve with the apple matchsticks, medlar jelly and a grating of fresh truffle.

Last Words on Medlar Jelly

Chef Jeremy Lee makes a tart glaze by melting medlar jelly in a small pan with a squeeze of lemon juice and drizzle over a poached pear and hazelnut galette. His recipe can be found on the *Guardian* website (www.theguardian.com). Bon appétit!

Medlar Cheese

Inexplicably, as I had never made jam or marmalade, my preserve making debut was tackling the random, ancient sounding recipe for medlar fruit cheese, which one of us had found on the internet.

It was autumn 2009, and I didn't know that I could freeze the bletted fruit, and postpone the making until I was under less self-imposed pressure to DO SOMETHING WITH THEM. My determination to make something, anything, with medlars, which were still a new discovery, has faded in my memory. I was over-confident, and it didn't go well.

With the benefit of hindsight, and a few ceiling splatters of exuberant medlar mixture, I assure you that medlar cheese is not difficult to make. It is time-consuming, and makes an ideal activity for a wet morning or afternoon, while you listen to something soothing.

It is worth the time, and medlar cheese has a set, grainy texture, and a fruity 'autumnal' flavour which encapsulates the medlar at its best, sweet at the front of the mouth with a light, astringent finish. My husband spreads it straight on to granary toast. He is the reason I first started making the fruit cheese. It keeps for ages, and is good to eat with a crunchy cheddar or a strong blue cheese. It also makes a fine stuffing for baked apples, when mixed with some additional spice, walnuts or hazelnuts, vine fruits and a little orange zest.

I make medlar cheese with three ingredients: medlar fruit pulp, granulated sugar and lemon juice. I gently dehydrate it over a low heat, stirring all the while to bring it to the setting consistency I am looking for. You can take it as far as you want, really: a butter, paste, or sliceable 'cheese'. The missing and unlisted ingredient is time. Fruit butter, as its name suggests is softly spreadable from the jar. Medlar paste is somewhat thicker and more concentrated, and spreadable. Medlar cheese is stiffer. If you dehydrate it to a very thick consistency, it may be set in a baking parchment lined loaf tin. It can be easily slipped out from the tin onto a piece of waxed paper, wrapped and stored. Take your pick.

This is how I make it.

Ingredients (make between eight and ten 100 g / 4 oz jars of
*   butter, paste or a soft set cheese)*
1 kg / 2 ¼ lbs medlar pulp, made with fresh or previously
*   frozen bletted medlars*
700 g / 1 ½ lbs granulated sugar
50 ml / 2 fl oz pure lemon juice

Tip the medlar pulp and pour the lemon juice into a preserving pan or a large, wide saucepan. Put the pan onto the stove and bring it up to a moderate heat. Weigh out the sugar and add it to the pan, stirring carefully with a long-handled spatula until it has dissolved into the fruity mass. The contents of the pan will be sloppy. Gradually bring it all up to boiling point. Now turn the heat down to a temperature which maintains a simmer. Stir the mixture regularly to prevent it from 'catching' on the base of the pan.

While this is going on, wash, rinse and oven dry your jars to sterilize them. Count out their lids. I set the oven to 150°C / 300°F / gas mark 2 and place an oven tray of the washed, drained and upright jars, not the lids, in there for 30 minutes, before turning off the heat. Leave the oven door closed.

The pulpy mixture gradually thickens, reduces in volume and dehydrates until it has reached the texture you're looking for. Don't leave the pan unattended. If you must briefly leave the room, turn the heat off before you go. To test for thickness, drag a silicon spatula or wooden spoon across the base of the pan, and when you see a clear channel left behind, you are ready to pot up the medlar cheese.

Remove the pan from the heat. Bring the sterilised jars to where you are going to fill them. Decant the contents of the pan into a spotlessly clean lipped pouring jug. Carefully ease the mixture into the jars with the help of a clean table knife and screw on the lids. I separately fill a ramekin with the leftover paste so that I can see how it looks and tastes when it is cool and set.

When the filled jars are tepid, give the lids another twist to tighten them off. Label and date. Store in a cool, dark place. Try to find small, straight sided, verrine style jars if you can. There is less waste and they look attractive on the table. They also make lovely presents and stocking fillers. People who like pears often, but not always, love medlar cheese. It may be the texture that wins them over.

Baked Apples with Spiced Medlar Cheese

This is another recipe from *The Norfolk Cook Book*. I make this towards the end of the Bramley apple harvest, by which time I'm looking for variations on an apple theme. I'm not strict about which nuts or seeds I add, nor am I fussy about the choice of citrus. I use what I have to hand.

Ingredient (serves 4)
4 medium sized Bramley apples, cored and unpeeled

1 x 100 g / 4 oz jar medlar cheese
40 g / 2 oz raisins or sultanas
20 g / 1 oz chopped walnuts, hazelnuts, or pumpkin seeds
small pinch ground cloves
½ tsp ground cinnamon
grated orange zest, as little or as much as you like

Preheat the oven to 180°C / 160°C fan / 350°F / gas mark 4. In a bowl, fork together the medlar cheese, dried fruit, chopped walnuts, ground cloves, cinnamon and orange zest, to your taste.

Pack a quarter of the mixture into the cavity of each apple. Score each one at its widest point and place them on a parchment or silicon lined baking sheet. Bake in the oven at 180°C (or 160°C fan) for 20 minutes.

Allow to cool slightly before serving with generous amounts of thick cream, ice cream, Greek yoghurt or vanilla custard.

Spicy Medlar Chutney

The next recipe is my interpretation of Pam Corbin's recipe for Spicy Medlar Chutney. When we were exchanging emails, she told me that this chutney was one of the recipes from her earliest TV episodes filmed with Hugh Fearnley -Whittingstall.

'Medlars are rather glorious fruits but they do need a certain understanding'. So true, Pam. And thank you for allowing me to include the recipe here.

This delicious chutney is packed with fresh garlic, ginger and chillies, and its warm fenugreek notes fragrantly remind me of the decades living in London's East End.

I wanted to emphasise the medlar flavour and texture, so I doubled the weight of medlar pulp and halved the quantity of apple. When I experimentally varied the ratios of medlar to apple, I left out the apple altogether in one version and replaced it with medlar pulp. It had an excellent flavour with all those wonderful spices and the fresh ingredients, and the texture was more akin to a paste, like a curry paste. There may be a place for this approach, as a base for a spicy chicken or butternut squash dish, but the feedback was to go with the version below.

At home, we eat this with cheese, cold meat and all kinds of curry. It is superb in a toasted cheese sandwich made with a blue cheese or cheddar. I swirl it through Greek yoghurt to make an instant dip to eat with poppadom. Spread onto granary bread in place of butter, it adds bite to a chicken (or turkey, pheasant, partridge…), lettuce and mayonnaise sandwich. It's wonderful with a top-notch pork pie or sausage roll.

Eastgate Larder Limited Edition Spicy Medlar Chutney

Ingredients

*1.4 kg / 3 lbs medlar pulp (from 2 to 2.5 kg / 4 ½ to 5 ½ lbs
    bletted medlars simmered briefly in 1.5 l / 2 ½ pints water)*

*700 g / 1 ½ lbs tart cooking apples cored and chopped. I use
    Bramleys.*

45 ml / 1 ½ fl oz light olive oil or other oil of your choice

4 tbsp mustard seeds

2 tbsp black peppercorns, crushed

½ tbsp fenugreek seeds

1 tbsp ground cumin

2 tsp turmeric

45 g / 1 ½ oz garlic peeled and grated

60 g / 2 oz fresh ginger grated. I don't peel it.

40 / 1 ½ oz finely chopped fresh red chillies (as hot as you like)
1 tbsp sea salt
500 g / 16 oz dark Muscovado sugar
500 ml / 17 ½ fl oz cider vinegar
225 ml / 8 fl oz medlar juice for topping up

Put the oil into a large, heavy-bottomed saucepan over a low heat. I use a large maslin preserving pan. Add the mustard seeds. When they begin to 'pop', add all the dry spices, and give them a good stir. Cook for 2 minutes.

Tip in the fresh garlic, ginger and chillies, stir into the mustard seeds and cook together for 2 minutes. Add the apples, mixing thoroughly with the spices.

Weigh the sugar into a large measuring jug and carefully pour over the vinegar to dissolve the muscovado. Pour the contents of the jug into the pan. Add the salt. Stir over low heat for another couple of minutes.

Now you're ready to add the medlar pulp, a ladleful at a time, stirring it in as you go until it has all been incorporated. Bring the pan up to the boil. Immediately reduce the heat and cook, uncovered, for about 2 hours, or until the mixture has thickened, stirring occasionally (add a little medlar juice if it looks too thick).

When you think it is ready, take a wooden spoon and drag it across the surface of the chutney. If it leaves a visibly shallow channel in its wake, it is ready to jar up. Turn off the heat, allow the chutney to cool very slightly then ladle into still warm, jars that have been sterilized in the oven at 150°C / 300°F / gas mark 2 for 30 minutes. (Fill the jars very full as the mix will shrink slightly when it cools).

Seal with new lids, label and store for six months to allow the chutney to mature before opening. This chutney keeps for ages, much longer than it takes us to eat it.

Medlar Creams

This recipe is adapted from *Quinces*, by Jane McMorland Hunter and Sue Dunster, inspired by Hannah Glasse's *The Art of Cookery Made Plain and Easy* (1747).

Quinces have more tartness to them than medlars so I've increased the quantity of medlar and slightly reduced the sugar. These are rich, so I make them in individual ramekins, leaving space for a handful of white currants, or a generous spoonful of gooseberry and elderflower compote.

Ingredients (serves 6)
250 g / 8 oz thick medlar pulp from sieving briefly simmered
  fruit
250 ml / 8 fl oz cream (single, double / heavy or mixed)
2 egg yolks
40 g / 1 ½ oz caster / fine sugar

Preheat the oven to 170°C / 340°F / gas mark 3. Beat the eggs yolks with the sugar until pale and thick. Beat in the cream. Fold in the medlar purée a little at a time, tasting as you add, until you have the flavour and texture you're looking for.

Butter six individual ramekins and pour in the mixture. Put the filled ramekins into a bain-marie and bake until set, about 40 minutes. Remove and chill. Covered, they will keep in the fridge for a couple of days.

Medlar Curd

This is well worth making, not only because it is lovely on sourdough toast, or swirled through good quality Greek or kefir yoghurt. It is a useful base for other things.

I use it to make salted medlar curd ice cream and a spin on millionaire's shortbread, where the caramel is replaced by the medlar curd. This is also adapted from a recipe in *Quinces*.

Ingredients (makes approx 500 g / 18 oz)
400 g / 14 oz medlar pulp, fresh or previously frozen
340g / 12 oz granulated sugar
juice of 1 lemon
75 g / 3 oz butter
2 eggs, lightly whisked

Put the pulp and the sugar in a solid based non-stick saucepan and heat gently to dissolve the sugar. Bring up to boiling point and reduce the heat. Simmer gently until the mixture pulls away from the sides of the pan. Incorporate the lemon juice with a whisk.

Still over a low heat, add the butter and stir until combined with the fruity mixture. It'll have a slight and pleasant texture to it.

Let it cool for a few minutes. Gradually add the whisked egg, beating it all together over the lowest heat possible. It will be glossy and smell divine.

Remove from the heat and pot up in warm, sterilized jars and seal. Store in the fridge after opening, where it will keep for a couple of months.

Salted Medlar Curd Ice Cream

This ice cream is a real surprise. It is delicious. It is quick and easy to make if you already have medlar curd in the fridge. Indeed, it is so good that making medlar curd is doubly worthwhile. And it doesn't need to be churned in an ice cream maker.

Ingredients
240 g / 8 oz medlar curd, recipe as above
250 ml / 8 fl oz double /heavy cream
¼ tsp sea salt
1 pinch sea salt flakes, to serve

Put the medlar curd in a large bowl and give it a good stir. Add a quarter of a teaspoon of salt and half of the cream, blending it into the curd. Add the rest of the cream and stir it in.

Scoop the mixture into an airtight container and freeze. Serve with a few flakes of sea salt sprinkled on top.

MILLIONAIRE'S MEDLAR SHORTBREAD

This is a real indulgence, an occasional treat in our house. It is based on a Felicity Cloake recipe. The medlar curd replaces the caramel.

Ingredients (makes about 24 squares)
For the shortbread:
200 g / 7 oz plain flour
100 g / 3 ½ oz medium cornmeal, semolina or rice flour
100 g / 3 ½ oz granulated sugar
¼ tsp fine salt
200 g / 7 oz butter, cut into pieces

For the topping:
500 g / 18 oz medlar curd (you may have some left over)
½ tsp fine salt
200 g / 7 oz dark chocolate (70% + cocoa solids)

Heat the oven to 180°C / 160°fan / 350°F / gas mark 4. Line a baking tin (about 20 x 20 cm / 8 x 8 in) with baking parchment, leaving an overhang.

Put the flour and cornmeal into a bowl with the sugar and salt. Mix well, cut in the butter and mix to form a dough. Press into the tin, prick all over with a fork and bake for about 25 to 30 minutes, until golden and crisp. Allow to cool.

Spread the medlar curd over the shortbread and smooth with a palette knife. Chill. Melt the chocolate in a heatproof bowl over a pan of simmering water or in a microwave, and spread evenly over the medlar curd. Leave until solid, then lift out of the tin and cut into squares.

Medlar and Walnut Loaf

Food journalist Xanthe Clay wrote that medlars are the English answer to the date. As mentioned elsewhere, Niki Segnit thinks of the medlar as 'a date that has sucked on a lemon'. I agree with them both. I don't tend to buy dates for baking with, I use bletted medlars or dip into my stash of frozen medlar pulp. Medlars are sweet, but nowhere near as sweet as dates. And they don't pack quite such an upward punch to our blood sugar levels.

They make this teatime medlar and walnut loaf, which is good on its own and even better spread with unsalted butter. It works well with strong cheese. Fruit cake, or an Eccles cake, eaten with cheddar is a 'thing', why not medlar and walnut loaf with Mrs Kirkham's Lancashire or a generous wedge of Montgomery's cheddar?

Ingredients
125 g / 4 ½ oz very soft, unsalted butter, cubed

200 g / 7 oz medlar pulp at room temperature mixed with a
   splash of water from a recently boiled kettle
150 g / 6 oz light soft brown sugar
2 large eggs
1 tsp baking powder
225 g / 8 oz self-raising flour
100 g / 3 ½ oz walnuts, roughly chopped

You need a 2 lb loaf tin (22 x 10 x 6 cm), lined with greaseproof baking parchment. Preheat the oven to 180°C / 160°C fan / 350°F / gas mark 4.

Put the butter and medlar pulp into a large bowl. With a wooden spoon, stir the ingredients together until there are no more lumps of butter. Whisk in the sugar until its smooth, then gradually incorporate the eggs until everything is combined. Add the baking powder and flour, plus the salt. Whisk again until the mixture is smooth and lump free. Fold in the walnuts. Spoon the mixture into the prepared loaf tin.

Bake for 20 minutes, then reduce the oven temperature to 170°C / 150 fan / 340°F / gas mark 3. Cook for another 45 to 50 minutes until the loaf is brown on top and a skewer inserted into the centre comes out clean. Rest the loaf in its tin for 15 minutes before removing it to a wire cake rack to cool down. Don't slice it until it has reached room temperature.

This loaf freezes well, whole or in slices, wrapped in foil, for up to three months.

PUDDINGS

Mark Diacono's affection for the medlar is as well known to readers of his articles, books and blogs, as it is to the thousands who follow him on social media. In the world of gardening, growing and cooking he's influential. Wise, enthusiastic and funny, he generously champions the forgotten and overlooked medlar.

About nineteen years ago, and newly moved to Otter Farm in Devon, Mark carefully selected those perennials, bushes and trees which would produce the kind of harvests that he and his family wanted to eat, and which were either expensive or unbuyable. Having met these criteria, a couple of dozen medlar trees, across a handful of cultivars, were settled into a corner of this idyllic seventeen-acre spot.

Mark has described the medlar's taste as 'like an apple had a child after an affair with a date', perfectly evoking the ingredient around which he created an unusual twist on an old favourite: sticky toffee pudding.

Mark's recipe appeared in one of his early books, *A Year at Otter Farm* (2014). With his enthusiastic agreement, and the kind permission of his publisher Bloomsbury, here it is, together with his introduction.

MEDLAR STICKY TOFFEE PUDDING

Other than the left-footed goal I scored from outside the box on the only time I played outfield for my primary school, this may be the pinnacle of my wintery achievements. You can be sure I wouldn't mess with something as perfect as a sticky toffee pudding and make it public if it wasn't special. Medlars' wonderful datey-ness pairs perfectly with the walnuts and the toffee to make this one of those wintery desserts that make the cold weather worth it. The brief grilling at the end is by no means essential, but it turns the top beautifully fudgy. I make a large preserving pan of medlar pulp and freeze it in 200 g quantities.

Ingredients (serves 6)
For the sauce:
125 g / 4 ½ oz unsalted butter
70 g / 2 ½ oz golden caster sugar
50 g / 2 oz dark muscovado sugar
150 ml / 5 fl oz double cream

For the cake:
200 g / 7 oz medlar pulp (simmer medlars with a little water
 until soft and sieve out the skins/seeds)
60 g / 2 ¼ oz unsalted butter, softened
85 g / 3 oz golden caster sugar
70 g / 2 ½ oz dark muscovado sugar
2 eggs
1 tsp bicarbonate of soda
180 g / 6 oz plain flour
1 tsp baking powder
1 tsp ground cloves
½ tsp salt
85 g / 3 oz walnuts, crushed

Preheat the oven to 180°C / 160°C fan / 350°F / gas mark 4. Lightly butter a baking dish approximately 24 x 20 cm / 9 ½ x 8 in.

Put the sauce ingredients in a pan, and heat gently until the butter melts. Turn the heat up and boil for 5 minutes, stirring frequently, until the sauce coats the back of a spoon. Pour a little over half of the sauce into the dish, allow to cool and refrigerate to firm up the sauce.

Beat the butter and sugars together, then add in the eggs, one at a time and beat until combined. Stir in the flour, baking powder, bicarbonate of soda, cloves and salt until incorporated. Thoroughly stir in the medlar pulp and the walnuts. Spoon the mixture into the dish, over the toffee sauce. Bake for 30 minutes.

Turn the grill on to a moderate heat. Make holes in the cake with a knife – just large enough to allow the sauce to soak in to the sponge – and pour over the remaining sauce. Grill for just long enough to crisp the top a little. Serve with a great deal of double cream or vanilla ice cream.

Roasted Medlars

These are easy and delicious to make, and slightly messy and sticky to eat. A good pudding to share with friends and family. Fingers may need to be called upon.

Ingredients
50 g / 2 oz butter
400 g / 14 oz medlars, bletted. This would work with
  previously frozen fruit.
75 g / 3 oz caster sugar
1 cinnamon stick

Heat the butter in an ovenproof frying pan and fry the medlars for 1 to 2 minutes. Add the sugar and cinnamon stick, then transfer the pan to the oven and roast for 10 to 15 minutes, or until the medlars are soft and the skins have split.

Serve with thick cream or vanilla ice cream.

Medlar Mincemeat

This is Sam Bilton's recipe, which was first published on her website in 2012. Thank you Sam for allowing me to include it here. Coincidentally, Sam is the author of two other Prospect Books volumes in the 'English Kitchen' series, *First Catch Your Gingerbread* (2020) and *Fool's Gold: A History of British Saffron* (2022).

We both favour Delia Smith's method of 'cooking' mincemeat at a very low temperature. The suet melts and coats the ingredients, sterilizing the mincemeat and prevents 'in glass' fermentation. And the possible jar explosions which could occur.

Ingredients (makes 3 x 450 g jars, or enough to fill 36 mince
   pies. Easy to scale up if extra supplies are needed)
200 g / 7 oz medlar purée
100 g / 3 ½ oz chopped mixed peel
100 g / 3 ½ oz dried cranberries
100 g / 3 ½ oz sultanas or raisins
100 g / 3 ½ oz currants
100 g / 3 ½ oz pitted dates, chopped
110 g / 4 oz vegetable suet
175 g / 6 oz soft dark brown sugar
finely grated zest and juice of 1 orange
finely grated zest and juice of 1 lemon
25 g / 1 oz blanched almonds cut into slivers
2 tsp mixed spice
¼ tsp ground cinnamon
a generous grating of nutmeg
3 tbsp Grand Marnier or Cointreau
1 tbsp brandy (or more if you like your mincemeat really boozy)

Mix all the ingredients together (except the alcohol) in a large, heat proof, non-metallic bowl or casserole. Cover with foil or a tight-fitting lid and leave overnight.

The next day preheat the oven to 120°C / 250°F / gas mark ½

(no higher). Place the covered bowl or casserole in the oven for 3 hours. Remove from the oven and intermittently stir well as the mincemeat cools. When the mincemeat is cool stir in the alcohol.

Spoon into sterilized jars, cover with waxed discs and seal. It should keep for several months in your larder but is probably best used within a year of production. (Truthfully, I have no idea how long it keeps as we rarely have any left beyond the end of December.)

Medlar Vinegar

I'm also grateful to Sam Bilton for her permission to include this recipe for medlar vinegar. You can use either whole bletted medlars for this recipe or medlar pulp if you have some left over from another recipe. Just lightly squash the whole fruit before you add the remaining ingredients.

Ingredients (makes approximately 4 x 350 ml bottles)
600 to 700 g / 1 ¼ to 1 ½ lbs medlar pulp or the equivalent
  weight of whole bletted medlars
1 litre / 35 fl oz white wine vinegar
450 to 750 g / 1 lb to 1 lb 10 oz granulated sugar
2 star anise
4 whole cloves
10 cm / 4 inch piece cinnamon stick

Steep the medlars in the vinegar for 3 to 5 days in a non-metallic container. Pour the contents into a jelly bag and allow to drain. This will take several hours so leave overnight if possible. DO NOT SQUEEZE the bag to get more liquid out otherwise your vinegar will be cloudy.

For every 600 ml / 1 pint vinegar add 450 g / 16 oz sugar (basically you need three quarters sugar to the quantity of vinegar). Put the vinegar, sugar and spices in a saucepan. Slowly bring to the boil then simmer for around 5 minutes removing any scum that floats to the surface.

Allow to cool then remove the spices and bottle. Use for salad dressings.

'THE MODEST MEDLAR'

You may already be familiar with *Cornucopia Magazine*, the magazine for connoisseurs of Turkey. It is published by Berrin Torolsan, who is a writer, photographer, and picture editor. In issue No. 60 I found her article 'The Modest Medlar', in which she waxes lyrical about 'this ambrosial amber-coloured fruit', encouraging her readers to take advantage of it wherever and whenever the opportunity presents itself.

I share her view that while eating medlars isn't very elegant, it is a sensuous experience. She advises: 'Snipping off the tiny stalk on top of the soft medlar, and holding the calyx at the bottom, peel back the thin, papery skin to reveal the pulp inside and suck it in, discarding calyx leaves and spitting out the five small stones.'

We exchanged emails, and she is kindly allowing me to reproduce the recipes from her article. I've selected four of the five, which are completely new to me, using, as they do, the fully grown and unbletted fruit: pickled medlar, medlar preserve, medlar cider and medlar vinegar.

Musmula Tursusu (Pickled Medlar)

This sweet-sour pickle is from Erzurum, in the north east-corner of

Turkey, and is a popular appetiser: easy to prepare, full of goodness and delicious with roasts, cold meats and rice *pilav*.

Ingredients
1 kg / 2.2 lbs medlars, fully grown and unbletted
½ tbsp salt
3 tbsp granulated sugar or honey
10 chickpeas, dried
1 bay leaf, optional

You will need a clean 3 litre jar with a lid. Rinse and trim the calyx and pierce each fruit once or twice with the tip of a knife. Choose a clean jar, add the chickpeas, then pack the medlars in, adding the bayleaf if you are using it. Fill the jar to the brim with water (to establish how much you need).

Pour the water into a mixing bowl. Add the salt and sugar (or honey) and mix well, stirring until completely dissolved. Return the liquid to the jar, place a weight on top of the fruit inside the jar, cover and leave to ferment in a dark, cool place. After two weeks the pickle is ready to be served.

Musmula Sirkesi (Medlar Vinegar)

This is an excellent vinegar, which I use wherever a recipe calls for the raw apple cider equivalent.

Ingredients
500 g / 1 lb medlars, unbletted
5 or 6 chickpeas, dried
½ tbsp rock salt
1 tbsp honey

½ glass vinegar, apple cider or wine

You will need a 2 litre jar with a lid. Wash the fruit and leave to drain and dry. Fill a jar with medlars, crushing them slightly as you add them. Add the chickpeas, salt, honey and vinegar.

Fill the jar with cold water, stir and cover. Stir daily until an opaque mould develops, then leave undisturbed to ferment.

When the vinegar turns acidic, after ten days or so, filter and decant into a bottle and leave to improve or until needed.

Musmula Marmeladi (Medlar Preserve)

This recipe is from Karacasu, a few miles from ancient Aphrodisias in western Anatolia. Medlars are rich in pectin and this amber preserve with its distinct aromatic, slightly tart flavour goes well with kaymak, or clotted cream, at breakfast or with hard cheese at any time.

My growing taste for the astringent flavour of unbletted medlar led me to make successive versions of this delicious preserve with five and ten percent less sugar. Its tartness complements full fat Greek yoghurt or homemade whole milk *kefir*, as well as creamy cheeses. This is a real winner and I look forward to making some each harvest time.

Ingredients
1 kg / 2.2 lbs medlars, hard or semi ripe
750 g / 1 lb 10 oz sugar
juice of half a lemon

You will need a large, wide pan and several jars with their lids, the jars sterilized and warm.

Rinse the medlars and place in your pan. Add water to cover and cook for about 20 minutes, until the fruit disintegrates. Remove from the heat. When it has cooled a little, press the pulp through a sieve into a bowl, including all the cooking liquid. Discard the pips and skins. Rinse out the pan. Transfer the contents of the bowl into the clean pan.

Add the sugar and simmer for 10 to 20 minutes, stirring from time to time until the preserve thickens. Add the lemon juice, increase the heat and bring to the boil once, then remove from the heat. While still hot, ladle into jars, screw the lids on tight and store in a cool, dark place until needed.

Tükenmez (Medlar Cider)

Other fruit from the kitchen and unbruised windfalls from the garden can all be added to this cider. It is traditionally made in *tükenmez* barrels, with a tap at the bottom, but any large jar can be used (a Kilner jar with a tap would work well).

In Berrin Torolsan's childhood, she remembers it as a fizzy, hay-coloured beverage, popular with everyone, young or old – a thirst quenching elixir well worth trying. Any cider consumed is replaced with the same amount of water, hence the name *tükenmez*, or 'never-ending.'

Ingtredients
1 kg / 2.2 lbs medlars, not too soft
1 bunch ripe grapes, any variety
2 quinces
2 or 3 apples
2 pears
1 or 2 tbsp sugar

Rinse the fruit and drain. Put the medlars and grapes to one side and roughly chop the rest of the fruit on a board without peeling or deseeding. Pack all the fruit into your chosen vessel. Add the sugar, cover with water, and place a lid on top.

Store in a cool, dark place to ferment for about a week, until it tastes sweet and slightly fizzy. When you start drinking it, replace the amount you have taken with the same quantity of water.

OLD MEDLAR RECIPES

Dorothy Hartley's *Food in England* (1954) includes a very short entry on the medlar, quoting from *The Child's Guide to Knowledge*, of 1850: 'Medlars are a native English fruit which grow wild in the hedges about Minishall in Cheshire. They are kept in moist bran for a fortnight before being rotten enough to eat.' Here are two of Hartley's suggestions for preparing and serving bletted medlars:

> [T]he brown squash within the rough skin is scraped out and mixed with cream and brown sugar.

> [A]rrange the medlars on a shallow dish with butter and cloves, and bake them a few minutes; serve like roasted apples.

STEWED MEDLARS

This is barely a recipe. Writing in 1536, the French botanist Jean Ruel described a type of *Mespilus* which had lost its thorns through cultivation and grafting. Once exposure to frost had removed the fruit's acerbity, it would be stewed with cinnamon in port wine, or other wine sweetened with honey, to make a conserve.

Preserving Medlars

An anonymous recipe published in London in 1653, described a method for preserving medlars:

> Take the fairest Medlers you can get, but let them not be too ripe, then set on faire water on the fire, and when it boyleth put in your Medlers, and let them boyle till they be somewhat soft, then while they are hot pill them, cut off their crowns, and take out their stones, then take to every pound of Medlers, three quarters of a pound of sugar, and a quarter of a pint of Rose water, seeth your Syrupe, scumming it clean, then put in your Medlers one by one, the stalks downward, when your Syrupe is somewhat cool then set them on the fire againe, let them boyle softly till the Syrupe be enough, then put in a few Cloves and a little Cinamon, and so putting them up in pots reserve them for your use.

Medlar Tart

Here are two ancient and two modern versions of medlar tart recipes. The first is taken from, though not attributed to, Thomas Dawson's *The Good Huswife's Jewel* (1585):

> Take Medlers that be rotten, and stamp them, and set them upon a chafin dish with coals, and beat in two yolks of Eggs, boyling till it be somewhat thick, then season it with Sugar, Cinnamon, and Ginger and lay it in paste.

This seems to have been the inspiration for this seventeenth-century recipe, from Robert May's *The Accomplisht Cook* (1660):

Take medlars that are rotten, strain them, and set them on a chaffing dish of coals, season them with sugar, cinamon, and ginger, put some yolks of eggs to them, let it boil a little, and lay it in a cut tart. Being baked, scrape on sugar.

Successful baking is a precise art, and I commend this modern interpretation, by Linda Duffin. Linda, a food and features writer living in our neighbouring county of Suffolk is the brains and talent behind Mrs Portly's Kitchen cookery school, which is based at her home. She's a member of the Guild of Food Writers and is an avid recipe developer. She is known for her interest in food history and has generously given me permission to include her recipe for a medlar tart. Thank you, Linda.

Medlar Tart

Rotten medlars. Doesn't sound very inviting, does it? And the old country name for these fruits was 'open arse', which while descriptive, is equally unappealing. It took me a long time to reconcile myself to medlars.

While you can make a medlar jelly from the freshly picked fruit, it is traditional to 'blet' them so that they soften and the flesh begins to break down. My father-in-law used to make a jelly from very well bletted medlars which had, to my palate, a really funky, rotten taste.

I've since discovered that you can blet them without taking them to such extremes. I put mine in a single layer in a wooden rack or basket somewhere cold and wait until they've softened and wrinkled, but rescue them before they get really manky. I suppose, like hanging pheasants, it is a matter of taste as to how far you take them.

A medlar is a very pretty tree when it is in blossom but apart from making jelly there aren't vast numbers of recipes for its fruit. One exception is Robert May's, quoted above. May was a Restoration cook and his book made early use of two ingredients brought to Europe from the Americas, turkey and potatoes.

I'm struck though by the similarity of his recipe to that US Thanksgiving classic, the pumpkin pie. I wonder if a version of the medlar tart crossed the Atlantic with early settlers and they adapted it to what was available locally?

My interpretation of May's recipe reflects this. While medlars, bletted or otherwise, aren't commonly available unless you know someone with a tree, this is a lovely autumn dessert and well worth a go if you can source some. It has a similar texture to pumpkin pie, but it is fresher and fruitier. I love it.

Ingredients (serves 6-8)
For the pastry:
240 g / 8 oz plain flour
pinch of salt
60 g / 2 oz white cooking fat
60 g / 2 oz butter
1 egg, lightly beaten
1 or 2 tbsp cold water

For the filling:
600 g / 21 oz (approx) bletted medlars (to give 300 g/ 10 oz
  purée)
1 tsp powdered ginger
1 tsp powdered cinnamon
a grating of nutmeg
100 g / 3 ½ oz soft light brown sugar

grated zest and juice of 1 orange and 1 lemon
2 eggs, well beaten

Prepping the bletted medlars is a bit fiddly and time-consuming so best done ahead of time. Remove the skins and pips and push the resulting gloop through a sieve so you have a smooth purée. Mix in the spices and set aside.

To make the pastry, either put the flour, salt and fats into a food processor and whizz until the mix resembles breadcrumbs or rub the fat into the flour with your fingertips. Add most of the beaten egg, reserving some for glazing. Cut it through until the pastry forms a ball and leaves the sides of the bowl clean. If it is too crumbly, add the cold water, a tablespoon at a time, until it comes together. Wrap and chill for 20 minutes.

Heat the oven to 200°C / 180°C fan / 400°F / gas mark 6.

Roll out around two-thirds of the pastry to line a greased, loose-bottomed 22 cm / 9 in flan tin, allowing a slight overhang. Use the remaining pastry to make decorations and brush with egg wash. Chill both for 20 to 30 minutes.

Trim the edges of the tart, line with foil and fill with baking beans. Blind bake for 15 minutes, then carefully remove the foil and beans. Brush the base with a little beaten egg and cook for another 5 to 10 minutes. Remove from the oven and set aside. Turn the oven down to 190°C / 170°C fan / 375°F / gas mark 5.

To make the filling, whisk together the sugar, fruit juices and spices until smooth. Add the zests and beaten eggs, then with a wooden spoon, beat in the medlar purée until smooth. Pour it into the tart base and cook for around 25 minutes until the filling is partly set, then remove the tart from the oven and apply your trimmings.

Put it back in for another 30 to 35 minutes, or until the pastry decorations are cooked and golden and a skewer inserted into the filling comes out clean. Allow to cool in the tin for 10 to 15 minutes before removing to a serving plate. I like to serve a bowl of tart crème fraîche alongside.

Spiced Medlar Tart With Walnut Pastry

The following recipes are reproduced here with the kind permission of their creator, Christine McFadden.

The pleasantly astringent flavour of this autumnal tart will have your friends guessing. Make sure the medlars are well bletted – the flesh should be dark orangey-brown and very soft.

The recipe looks long but can easily be broken down into manageable parts. For example, you can deal with the pastry the day before. You can also make the filling in advance and keep it in the fridge.

Ingredients for the pastry (serves 6-8)
55 g / 2 oz shelled walnuts
150 g / 5 ½ oz plain flour
55 g / 2 oz caster sugar
a pinch of salt
75 g / 2 ¾ oz butter, chilled and diced
2 egg yolks, lightly beaten
1½ to 2 tbsp cold water

For the filling:
850 g / 1 lb 14 oz bletted medlars
3 eggs, lightly beaten
150 ml / 5 fl oz single cream
75 g / 2 ¾ oz caster sugar
½ tsp ground cinnamon

½ tsp ground ginger
¼ tsp nutmeg, freshly grated
¼ tsp salt
1 tbsp lemon juice
walnuts small handful roughly chopped, to decorate
icing sugar sieved, to decorate
whipped cream to serve

To make the pastry, first finely grind the walnuts using a food processor or Nutribullet. Next, sift the flour into a bowl, then mix in the sugar, ground walnuts and salt. Rub in the diced butter until the mixture looks like fine breadcrumbs. Stir in the egg yolks and water, and lightly mix to a dough. Roll into a ball, then flatten to form a thick disc. Wrap in greaseproof paper (not cling film) and chill for 30 minutes.

Lightly grease the base and sides of a fluted shallow 23 cm / 9 in tart tin with a removable base. Make sure the sides are well lubricated. Roll the pastry disc thinly into a circle and carefully lift it into the tin. Press it well into the sides with the edge of your index finger. Trim the top with a sharp knife and use the off-cuts to reinforce any weak areas. Chill for 30 minutes.

Preheat the oven to 190°C / 170°C fan / 375°F / gas mark 5. Prick the pastry base with a fork and line with foil and baking beans. Bake for 15 minutes, then remove the foil and beans and bake for 5 minutes more. Remove from the oven and leave to cool.

Meanwhile, slice the medlars in half horizontally. Scrape out the flesh, discarding the seeds. Push through a coarse sieve, pressing hard with the back of a wooden spoon. Scrupulously scrape the outside of the sieve to remove every bit of flesh. You will need about 350 g / 12 oz.

Set the oven temperature to 180°C / 160°C fan / 350°F / gas mark 4.

Put the flesh in a blender with the eggs and cream. Combine the sugar, spices and salt in a small bowl. Add this to the medlar mixture along with the lemon juice, then whizz to a smooth purée.

Pour the purée into the pastry case. Bake for 45 to 50 minutes, rotating the tin halfway through, until a knife tip inserted in the centre comes out clean.

Leave to cool then sprinkle with chopped walnuts followed by a dusting of icing sugar.

Medlar and Ginger Creams

The pleasantly sharp flavour of medlars is delicious mixed with cream and spices. Serve with crisp Langue du chat biscuits.

Ingredients (serves 4)
650 g / 1 lb 6 oz bletted medlars
1½ tbsp finely chopped stem ginger
4 tbsp ginger syrup from the jar
175 ml / 6 fl oz apple juice
1½ tbsp lemon juice
125 ml / 4 fl oz whipping cream or double cream
stem ginger slivers to decorate

Slice the medlars in half horizontally. Scrape out the flesh, discarding the seeds. Push through a coarse sieve, pressing hard with the back of a wooden spoon. Scrupulously scrape the outside of the sieve to remove every bit of flesh. You will need about 225 g.

Mix the flesh with the chopped ginger, the syrup from the ginger jar, plus the apple juice and lemon juice.

Whip the cream for 3 to 4 minutes until just firm, then swirl this into the medlar mixture. Spoon into small individual serving bowls and chill for an hour or two.

Just before serving, decorate with a few very thin slivers of stem ginger.

Variation

Replace the ginger elements with 1 ½ tablespoons of acacia honey and 1 teaspoon of ground cinnamon. Decorate with a drizzle of honey and a few slivers of almonds.

ALCOHOL

Steeping Medlar Spirits… and Brewing

If you want to make medlar alcohol, either by steeping them in gin or brandy, or making beer, please, please always use newly bletted fruit. Steeping in spirits is best done with medlars that are just shy of being one hundred percent bletted, when there is still a thin, pale layer of flesh under the skin. With practice, you can feel when they've softened sufficiently. This was the most welcome advice offered to me by a seasoned 'steeper' over a glass of her quince liqueur. I had just about recovered from the disastrous and expensive mistake I had made a few months earlier, using previously frozen fruit and had been close to giving up altogether on making medlar gin. Freezing the fruit is absolutely fine as a storage method if you're going to bake, make preserves or ice cream. The fruit's cell walls break down a bit during the freezing process, which is fine for cooking. However, the cells' breakdown causes excessive and unattractive cloudiness, especially in spirit steeps.

I did it just the once, and the result was horrible. The gin steep had given up a significant percentage of the starting alcohol content to the fruit. When it was time to take medlars to the foraging brewer I work with, usually a cheery fellow, he reported a serious mash tun pipe blockage caused by medlar sludge. His pipework recovered and happily we are still friends. I now take him crates of newly harvested, unbletted medlars and he monitors their progress until he's ready to brew with them. The results are impressive: a bitter with a toffee apple finish and an abv. somewhere north of six percent. This year he experimented further by placing smaller batches of the medlar bitter in port, whisky or bourbon casks. These beers are unique accompaniments to cheese and charcuterie, to be enjoyed like wine. They range in abv. from just under 9% to nearly 12%.

I have written elsewhere about the trials and tribulations I encountered on the way to producing the first commercial batch of Norfolk Medlar Gin Liqueur in 2021, a project which was several years in development. It has to be defined as a 'gin liqueur' because the abv is lower than the minimum 37.5% required by UK law for it to be simply called 'gin.'

Fruit spirit steep recipes recommend the addition of sugar. This makes sense if you are using sloe, rhubarb or raspberry fruit. If you have got this far into the story, the medlar's intrinsic sweetness will be familiar to you. And when I tried steeping medlars in quality gin with added sugar, it tasted like sickly overkill.

Medlar fruit steeped in Norfolk Gin produces a dry 'gin liqueur', with an abv. of just under 30% and a glorious light straw colour, just a few shades deeper than the original gin, which is a pale shade of cardamom. It is good over ice, with a twist of orange peel, in a gin and tonic (use good quality tonic) with thyme and lime. Last but not least, it makes a very fine cocktail with a quality sparkling white wine. We're fortunate in Norfolk that several vineyards are producing very fine examples of these, so I can really keep it local.

To steep successfully, the medlars themselves must be newly harvested and no more than ninety-five percent bletted. The flesh just under the skin should still be pale, surrounding the sweet brown bletted interior. It will be slightly firmer, which helps minimise the cloudiness created by soft squishy fruit, but still enabling the exchange of flavour between the spirit and the fruit.

I use spotlessly clean 8 litre Kilner jars, in which I put about 1 ½ kg fruit and 6 litres of Norfolk Gin. I close the lids, and set them aside somewhere cool and dark. I wait until the gin tastes right to me. This will take anywhere between six and twelve weeks.

I strain off the fruit through a capacious 30 cm / 12 in diameter, fine mesh sieve lined with muslin into spotlessly clean lipped jugs. Then I filter the gin and decant it into storage containers before abv testing and bottling.

The fruit is boozy and fruity, delicious as an alcohol-packed after-dinner treat. I store some in the fridge just for this. Probably something for the medlar diehards among you.

This is a process, not a recipe. It is worth a go if you have a really good gin that you like enough to experiment with. It may be a 'winter gin' with definable spice notes. Or a citrussy one. Have a go with half a bottle of spirit and a handful of medlars. I'm always happy to chat, if you'd like to talk it through.

Tips and Hints

Here are my tips for getting the most out of a medlar tree, based on my experience and the questions I am frequently asked.

A Bare Root or Pot Grown Tree?

Medlars are undemanding of a busy gardener, requiring relatively little in the way of pruning. It is best to buy a grafted bare root, one or two-year-old tree. Think about the planting situation and choose a rootstock to suit. Keepers Nursery offers this service.

Recommended Cultivars

— 'Iranian' and 'Nottingham' have a good flavour and texture for the table.
— 'Nottingham' for all round usefulness and flavour.
— 'Dutch' and 'Large Russian' for their large size, less appealing as a table fruit.
— 'Flanders Giant', 'Macrocarpa', 'Breda', 'Bredase Reus' and 'Royal' all have a good flavour.

Situation, Soil and Planting

A sheltered, sunny spot in well-drained neutral to slightly acid soil is preferred. Our trees were planted in square holes, to which we added leaf mould and garden compost, a handful of fish, blood and bone and a bucket of water. They were staked and tied in. The planting area was topped off with a square metre of water permeable grass and weed suppressant matting. This was removed after three years, once the roots were well down. Then we started mulching with a mix of garden compost, leaf mould and woodchip.

Establishing And Watering

Water during prolonged dry spells in the first three years. The leaves will flop and tell you if water is required. Water with a hose for about a minute into the ground alongside the stake. Don't let the tree fruit until the second summer after planting.

Pollination

Any pollinators will do the job. The flowers appear in May, and provide landing pads for honey bees, flies, wasps, hoverflies, bumbles etc.

When to Harvest

Medlar fruit takes about five months to fully grow. I look for the following from the third week of October (April in the southern hemisphere): changing leaf colour to yellow, orange, red and brown; leaf fall; hard, fully grown fruit lying on the ground; lots of fruits falling to the ground when you shake the tree. Last of all, cooling but not necessarily freezing, night temperatures.

Medlar fruit will eventually blet on the tree, and they are much harder to pick when they are soft. I usually complete the harvest of the hard, fully grown, and ready to pick ones by mid-November.

Bletting

This is the naturally occurring process by which the hard, astringent and tannic flesh ripens from the inside out. It usually, but not always, happens off the tree, and takes anything between a few days and a couple of weeks. The fruit darkens and softens, it smells and tastes distinctly sweet so pull one apart and taste it, avoiding the five stones. They are fully blettted when they are brown all the way through. Try to mimic nature by choosing a well ventilated, cool space. Left to their own devices on the tree, medlars will naturally blet, eventually. If you have picked fully grown fruit, the little stem attaching the fruit to the tree will no longer show any green in the middle.

Storing

Medlars will keep in the cool for a few weeks. In the past they would have been stored in sand or straw, or in an ice room if available. They may be frozen in zip lock plastic bags when bletted. If you choose fruit to serve as a table fruit at a later time, they are best frozen separately on a baking sheet before packing them into zip lock plastic bags.

Cooking and Eating

Top notch, freshly bletted medlars make an unusual table fruit, served with cheese and wine. For cooking, bletted fruit is usually used. Medlar jelly and medlar fruit cheese complement cheese, furred and feathered game, poultry, charcuterie, lamb and pork. Unbletted fruit can be used to make pickles, tangy preserves, vinegar and cider.

Medlars may be steeped in spirits. They make syrup, jam, jelly, fruit pastes, fruit cheese, chutneys, vinegar, cakes, tarts, steamed puddings, custards, ice cream and tart fillings. The whole bletted fruit may be baked with spices and served with cream.

Pectin Anyone?

Unbletted medlars have loads of pectin, bletted ones don't. Two-thirds bletted to a third unbletted when boiling them to make jelly really helps. As does lemon juice in the jelly making stage. Jam and preserving sugars make bouncy preserves, at least in my hands they do, so I never use them.

WHERE TO BUY MEDLAR TREES

UK

Ashridge Trees, Chris Bowers & Sons, Keepers Nursery, Mail Order Trees, Frank P. Matthews, Orange Pippin Trees, Pomona Fruits, Victoriana Nursery.

USA

Cricket Hill Garden, Connecticut; Englands Orchard & Nursery, Kentucky; Fedco Trees, Maine; One Green World, Portland, Oregon; Planting Justice, California; Raintree Nursery, Washington State; Trees of Antiquity, California; Ty Ty Nursery, Georgia.

CANADA

Carson's Garden and Market, Ontario; Vancouver Fruit Trees and More, Vancouver; Whiffletree, Ontario.

AUSTRALIA

Woodbridge Fruit Trees, Tasmania. Bulleen Art Garden, Victoria; Heritage Fruit Trees, Victoria; Rayners Orchard, Victoria; Yalca Fruit Trees, Victoria; Daleys Fruit, NSW; Guildford Garden Centre, WA.

NEW ZEALAND

Edible Garden Co, Palmerston North; Southern Woods Nursery, Christchurch; Kaipaki Nursery and Orchard, Waikato.

Acknowledgements

This book is dedicated to the core of people without whose presence, love and friendship I couldn't imagine a medlar orchard, a business or a book.

At the centre of this core is my husband David, and our family. The decision to make our life in Norfolk was easy. In 2012 we finally achieved it, after searching for a home with space inside and out for our blended brood of seven adult children. They planted our first medlar trees for us as an ornamental avenue in the winter of 2012-13.

Marrying David was my best decision, living here came a close second. Thank you, darling, for everything, and for wanting to live in Norfolk.

I had no idea that locating within the catchment area for the Norfolk and Norwich University Hospital would become so significant. It certainly spared me from invasive medical treatment in 2015, for which I profoundly thank the hospital's wonderful gastroenterology team. Thank you to everyone who cared for me, especially surgeon Chris Speakman and the team of specialist nurses. Royalties from sales of this book will go directly to the N&N Hospitals Charity.

My thanks go to Mike Simpson of Mail Order Trees, for supplying ninety thriving 'Nottingham' medlars, to guarantee a supply of fruit for my little business.

Hamid Habibi of Keepers Nursery, grower and supplier of other medlar cultivars, is sadly no longer with us. Of course, I would like to thank him, and you, Karim, for all your experience and insight which you shared with me in the early days of the business, and while I was getting to grips with the number of medlar trees that are actually bought in the UK.

My deep appreciation to you, Janet Sleep, chair of Norfolk Plant Heritage, for your enthusiasm about the young medlar orchard, and for your patient guidance and sponsorship of my application for the trees to become a National Collection. I'm so pleased that Norfolk has its first Collection of trees, and with it, an amenity for people to visit. You and your colleagues are always welcome here.

I would like to thank my publisher, Catheryn Kilgarriff, and her editor, Brendan King for steering this nervous novice through the process of bringing the medlar to life in book form. I must thank David again too; you quietly embarked on a vast body of meticulous and authoritative medlar research and delivered it straight into my lap. Thank you. David undertook this for its own merit and to satisfy his curiosity about the medlar, while I was physically and mentally elsewhere, focusing on my family during a tricky time.

Thank you, Simon Greenwood, for everything you bring to Eastgate: gardening skills, several thousand honeybees, your knowledge and experience which are of incalculable value to this amateur. You have helped transform these acres in the few years that you have been here. Oh, how we laugh about wayward medlar trees, interfering with mowing the grass so it is manageable for harvest. Thank you for your patience with all of us.

Jenny Boag, thank you so much for introducing me to nearby established medlar trees in the autumn of 2016, when I urgently needed to locate additional fruit. I deeply value our friendship, and appreciate your support and enthusiasm for the medlar orchard, as well as recounting the tales of your own happy years at Eastgate. You set a lively ball rolling, and now I know 70 garden owners with a medlar tree, mostly around east and south Norfolk, and my thanks go to each and every one of you who have annually contributed fruit in exchange for charity donations since 2016.

My eternal thanks go to my thinking partner, Chris Arnheim,

for our weekly hour on the phone, which enables us, individually and effectively, to generate ideas, problem solve and rehearse difficult conversations in a safe and non-judgmental space. There were plenty of these this year, and I'd have been lost without you during the blockages and the periods of intense writing. Thank you so much.

Which brings me to Sarah Pettegree. Thank you for your friendship, your wisdom, and your practical generosity to me and the medlar orchard, especially at harvest time. Thank you for agreeing to be my 'ordinary reader' (what IS this expression?). You kindly waded through the first iteration of the stitched together chapters, and so sensitively talked me through your thoughtfully considered, annotated and detailed comments. There's nothing at all ordinary about your contribution, thank you for taking such care.

Thanks also to you, we have had fun hosting Catherine Phipps' pressure cooking demo evenings here in the Eastgate kitchen. Our lovely friendship with Catherine has shone a light onto fellow cookery authors, Annie Gray and Mark Diacono, hitherto unmet, who LOVE medlars. They have known the fruit far longer than I have; thank you both for your encouragement, advice and enthusiasm for this passionate upstart's medlar world.

Catherine, thank you for your perceptive advice and thoughtful support while I was getting my mind around starting the book in the first few weeks of this year. I was fearful, and you calmed me, by generously listening during our time together in Norfolk as the year unfolded.

New pals, each of them food writers with a side interest in medlars, Linda Duffin and Sam Bilton, have collided with me, via social media, and I would like to thank you both for your warmth and friendliness, and your permission to include your own stories and recipes in the book. It's so refreshing to hear voices other than mine in the recipes.

Sarah, you are a true maven, suggesting to Tim Maddams that he might want to record a medlar focused podcast with me. Thank you, Tim, for the chance to laugh excessively during our recording. And my thanks for your thoughts on an embryonic introduction to the book which I lobbed at you, which was well caught, and beautifully returned.

Thank you again Sarah, for introducing me to Jonathan and Alison Redding, who have become good pals. Bumpily, but eventually, Norfolk Medlar Gin Liqueur was born. Thank you Mr. and Mrs. Redding for your patience with the medlar, which so hates being rushed.

My middle daughter Ellie, founder and creative director of AveDesignStudio (which is named after my late mother, Averil), blended Norfolk Gin's and Eastgate Larder's black and white brand designs to convey what is in a 'medlar gin' bottle: Norfolk Gin with a medlar accent. Ellie had taken me on the journey to develop a brand for Eastgate Larder in 2016, interrogating every aspect and detail of the product, thinking about taste, colour and how to avoid product waste by choosing straight sided little jars. Thank you, Ellie, the work you and your colleagues did for me is admired and appreciated by me whenever I am labelling, and each time the jars meet someone new.

Lou and Lottie, my eldest and youngest daughters. Thank you, Lou, for your dependably thorough internet searches which confirmed that a dedicated medlar fruit business didn't already exist, when my vague feeling started to take on a shape in 2015. And Lottie, your enthusiasm for preserve making is a joy; I love our time together in the kitchen working on your favourite and new flavours. You make the process seem new and exciting, every time.

Thank you, Jane Dalton, for finding me at the 2017 Norfolk Show and inviting me to talk about the medlar to your village's gardening club. Your confidence has led to many similar opportunities, and I hope that these lovely evenings will continue. Over the years, they have raised funds for Thornage Hall. Recently, sales proceeds and speaking fees have gone to support small groups of Ukrainian refugees in Poland.

I met Julia Platt Leonard at my stall outside Pistachio&Pickle in London's Camden Passage in 2017. Thank you, Julia, for your immediate interest in the weird medlar, and for quickly following up with an article about it in the Independent. Later, when the orchard was promoted to a National Collection, you pounced on Country Life magazine and wrote a second piece. I'm so grateful for your enthusiasm, and your warmth, it was a pleasure getting to know you through working with you on these, thank you.

An enormous and heartfelt thank you goes to all the independent delis and cheese shops which are so valuable to Eastgate Larder and me, and which are trusted in turn by their customers to bring them provenance, flavour and quality in all the products they stock. The medlar's fortunes are gradually transforming because of your individual and combined commitment to stocking my little jars. Thank you, each and every one of you, present and past.

Please take a bow: Earsham St Deli, Slate Cheese, Norfolk Deli, Back to the Garden, Norfolk Cheese Company, Jarrolds, St. Giles' Pantry, Fen Farm Dairy, Burwash Larder, Pinney's of Orford, Flint Vineyard, Old Hall Farm, Holkham Hall, Star Plain Stores, Walsingham Farms Shop, G.F. White Butchers, Aaron Christie, Picnic-Fayre; The High St Deli, Jericho Cheese, Cotswold Cheese, Neal's Yard Dairy, the Giddy Grocer, General Store, Melrose & Morgan, Scott's of Alnwick, No. 2 Pound St., Partridges of Sloane Square, Thackray Brown, The Farm, Stratford, E.J. Proudfoot, Cairn Distillery, Laura's Larder, Diane's Pantry, The Goring Grocer, The Tuscan Farm Shop, Eve's Hill Farm, Pangbourne Cheese Shop, Jigsaw Bakery.

Thank you, Mike Deal, for bringing the medlar to your Wildcraft Brewery fans, many of whom may not have met this odd autumn fruit. Your beer is a triumph. Thank you for persevering!

My thanks and gratitude to Simon and Nicola Rawcliffe for your help and advice when I was navigating the HMRC and the onerous (to me) licence application to make and wholesale medlar gin. I couldn't have done it without you, thank you.

Helen Allen, thank you so much for accepting David's commission to paint the medlar through all its seasons. I'm thrilled that it graces the book's cover.

Cheryl Roux, thank you for all your interest and encouragement in the years we have known one another. My thanks Liz Macann for introducing us.

I must thank chef Richard Bainbridge for connecting me, via a greengrocer, with two beautiful medlar trees in Sheringham; thank you, Rob Walpole, for putting your delicious home grown medlar jelly on your menu, and for your kind words about mine. To Marie Paule of Chez Rosito in Paris, 'je vous remercie de vos conseils au sujet de la liqueur de fruit.'

I have loved food writing since I was a teenager, discovering Elizabeth David and Jane Grigson around my eighteenth birthday, and revelling in their evocative language which I instantly saw and felt in my imagination. The bibliography includes more of my favourite writers, so I won't repeat them here.

I'd like to thank my followers on social media, who are mostly, but not exclusively connected with food, gardens and farming. This huge group includes friends I've met in real life, especially Jacob Ikareth of Hobart, Will Tatchell of Van Dieman Brewing near Launceston, Tasmania and Gerit Quealy of New York and Washington. I'll be seeing you, hopefully in 2023-24, with copies of the book.

BIBLIOGRAPHY

Allan, Mea. *The Tradescants: Their Plants, Gardens and Museum, 1572-1662* (London: Michael Joseph, 1964).

Allen, D. *Forgotten Skills of Cooking* (London: Kyle Books, 2009).

Alleton, V. and Lackner, M. (eds). *De l'un au multiple: Traduction du chinois vers les langues européennes* (Paris: MSH, 1999).

Amherst, Alicia. *A History of Gardening in England* (London: Quaritch, 1895).

Badenes, M.L., Janick, J., Lin S., Zhang, Z., Liang, G.L., Wang, W. 'Breeding Loquat', *Plant Breeding Reviews*, Vol. 37, 2013.

Baird, J., and Thieret, J. 'The medlar (*Mespilus germanica, Rosaceae*) from antiquity to obscurity', *Economic Botany*, Vol 43, No 3, 1989: 328–372.

Bakels, C. and Jacomet, S. 'Access to Luxury Foods in Central Europe during the Roman Period', *World Archaeology*, Vol 34, No.3, 2003.

Bauman, J. 'Tradition and Transformation: The Pleasure Garden in Piero de' Crescenzi's *Liber ruralium commodorum*', *Studies in the History of Gardens and Designed Landscapes* (Summer 2002), 22: 99-141.

Beresford, J. (ed). *The Diary of a Country Parson, 1758-1802 by James Woodforde* (London: Canterbury Press, 2011).

Bergara, Liza. *Makhila* (Montreuil: Gourcuff Gradenigo, 2021).

Berners, Dame J. *A Treatyse of Fysshynge wyth an Angle*, with an introduction by Rev. M.G. Watkins M.A. (London: Elliot Stock, 1880).

Blanc, Raymond. *The Lost Orchard* (London: Headline, 2019).

Bodart-Bailey, B., and Massarella, D. *The Furthest Goal: Engelbert Kaempfer's Encounter with Tokugawa Japan* (London: Routledge, 1995).

Botfield, B.(ed). *Manners and Household Expenses of England in the Thirteenth and Fifteenth Centuries* (London: William Nicol, 1841).

Boulger, G.S. *Familiar Trees* (London: Cassell and Co., 1907).

Boulger, G.S. *Wood: A Manual of the Natural History and Industrial Applications of the Timbers of Commerce* (London: Edward Arnold, 1902).

Browicz, K. 'Distribution of woody *Rosaceae* in W. Asia II', *Arboretum Kórnickie* (1973) 13:27-36.

Cecil, E. *A History of Gardening in England* (London: Quaritch, 1896).

Cevahir, G., and Bostan, S.-Z. 'Organic Acids, Sugars and Bioactive

Compounds of Promising Medlar (*Mespilus germanica*) Genotypes Selected from Turkey', *International Journal of Food Science*, 2021, 21(45):1-11.

Chambers, W. and R. *Chambers's Edinburgh Journal*, Vol. XVII (London: W.S. Orr, 1852).

Clay, Xanthe. 'There's more to medlars than meets the eye', *Daily Telegraph*, 21 October 2016.

Corbin, P. *Preserves: River Cottage Handbook No. 2* (London: Bloomsbury, 2008).

Cobbett, William. *The American Gardener* (Montana: Kessinger, 2007).

Cockayne, O. *Leechdoms, Wortcunning, and Starcraft of Early England*, Vol. II (London: Longman, Green, Longman, Roberts and Green, 1864-6).

Crawford, M. with Aitken, C. *Food From Your Forest Garden* (Cambridge: Green Books, 2013).

Cristofori, V., Silvestri, C., Pica, A.L., Bertazza, G. 'Evaluation of Medlar Cultivars: agronomical, pomological and qualitative traits', *European Journal of Horticultural Science* (2019) 84, 6:350-358.

Culpeper, Nicholas. *The English Physitian Enlarged* (London: John Streater, 1666).

Diacono, Mark. *A Year at Otter Farm* (London: Bloomsbury, 2014).

— *A Taste of the Unexpected* (London: Quadrille Publishing, 2010).

— *Fruit: River Cottage Handbook No. 9* (London: Bloomsbury, 2011).

— *Grow & Cook: The Ultimate Kitchen Garden Guide* (London: Headline, 2020).

Dickson, C. 'Macroscopic fossils of garden plants from British Roman and medieval deposits', in *Garden History: Species, Forms and Varieties from Pompeii to 1800,* edited by D. Moe *et al* (Belgium: PACT, 1994).

Dioscorides. *De materia medica* (South Africa: Ibidis Press, 2000).

Dunn, Stephen T. *Alien Flora of Britain* (London: West, Newman & Co., 1905).

Eaton, M. *The Cook and Housekeeper's Dictionary* (Bungay: J. and R. Childs, 1822).

Ellis, W. *The Timber-Tree Improved* (London: Osborne and Cooper, 1744).

Evelyn, John. *Directions for the Gardiner and Other Horticultural Advice* edited by M. Campbell-Culver (Oxford: Oxford University Press, 2009).

Evelyn, John. *Silva: or, A Discourse of Forest-Trees,* with notes by A. Hunter (York: Wilson and Spence, 1801).

Evreinoff, V.A. 'Notes sur l'origine, la biologie et les variétés du néflier', *La Revue Horticole* (1953) 125: 976-979.

Facaros, D. and Pauls, M. *Bilbao and the Basque Lands* (London: New Holland Publishers, 2012).

Fish, D.T. *Cassell's Popular Gardening* (London: Cassell, 1884).

Fitch, J.G. (tr). *Palladius: The Work of Farming (Opus Agriculturae) and Poem on Grafting* (London: Prospect Books, 2013).

Fortenbaugh, W., Huby, P., Sharples, R., Gutas, D. *Theophrastus of Eresus. Sources for His Life, Writings, Thought and Influence* (Leiden: Brill, 1993).

Freeman, Margaret B. *The Unicorn Tapestries* (New York: Dutton, 1976).

Gerard, John. *The Herball* (London: John Norton, 1597).

Glasse, Hannah. *The Art of Cookery Made Plain and Easy* (London, 1747).

Googe, B. (tr). *Four bookes of husbandry collected by M. Conradus Heresbachius* (London: John Wight, 1578).

Gray, Dr A. *The Greedy Queen: Eating with Victoria* (London: Profile Books, 2017).

Greco, G.L. and Rose, C.M. (tr). *The Good Wife's Guide (Le Ménagier de Paris): A Medieval Household Book* (Ithaca and London: Cornell University Press, 2009).

Grigson, Jane. *Jane Grigson's Fruit Book* (London: Michael Joseph, 1982).

Grindon, L.H. *British and Garden Botany* (London: Routledge, Warne, and Routledge, 1864).

Gunther, R.T. *Early British Botanists and their Gardens* (Oxford, Oxford University Press, 1922).

Hadfield, M. 'Trees and Their Periods: Some Notes on Arboricultural Planting in the British Isles', *Garden History,* Vol 4, No 2 (Summer, 1976): 23-29.

Hammond, E. *Modern Domestic Cookery, and Useful Receipt Book* (London: Dean and Munday, 1819).

Hamy, P.A. *Entrevue de François Premier avec Henry VIII à Boulogne-sur-Mer, en 1532* (Paris: Lucien Gougy, 1898).

Hartley, D. *Food in England* (London: Macdonald & Jane's, 1954).

Harvey, John. *Mediaeval Gardens* (London: Batsford, 1990).

— 'Garden Plants of Moorish Spain: A Fresh Look', *Garden History*, Vol. 20, No. 1 (Spring, 1992): 71-82.

— 'Westminster Abbey: The Infirmarer's Garden', *Garden History*, Vol. 20, No. 2 (Autumn, 1992): 97-115.

Henderson, P. 'Sir Francis Bacon's Essay 'Of Gardens' in Context', *Garden History,* Vol. 36, No. 1 (Spring, 2008): 59-84.

Henry, D. *Salt, Sugar, Smoke* (London: Mitchell Beazley, 2012).

Heresbach, C. *Rei rusticae libri quatuor* (Cologne: Birckmann, 1570).

[Hill, Georgiana]. *Foreign Desserts for English Tables* (London: Richard Bentley, 1862).

Historical Manuscripts Commission, 'Liber albus I: Fols. 161-80', in *Calendar of the Manuscripts of the Dean and Chapter of Wells: Vol. 1* (London, 1907).

Hogg, Robert. *The Fruit Manual* (London: Cottage Gardener Office, 1860).

Horn, W. and Born, E. *The Plan of St. Gall* (Berkeley: University of California Press, 1979).

Janick, J. and Paull, R.E. (eds). *The Encyclopedia of Fruit and Nuts* (Wallingford: CABI Publishing, 2008).

Jessen, C., (ed). *Alberti Magni ex ordine praedicatorum de Vegetabilibus libri VII, historiae naturalis pars XVIII* (Berlin: Berolini, typis et inpensis Georgii Reimeri, 1867).

Johnson, G.W. *A History of English Gardening* (London: Baldwin & Cradock, 1829).

Jones, Sir H.S. and McKenzie, R. *A Greek-English Lexicon by H. G. Liddell and R. Scott* (Oxford: Clarendon Press, 1940).

Ladd, C.A. 'The 'Rubens' Manuscript and Archbishop Ælfric's Vocabulary, *Review of English Studies*, Vol. 11, No. 44, (1960): 353-364.

Lebo, K. *The Book of Difficult Fruit* (New York: Farrar, Straus and Giroux, 2021).

Lev-Yadun, S. and Weinstein-Evron, M. 'Late Epipalaeolithic Wood Remains from El-Wad Cave, Mount Carmel, Israel', *New Phytologist*, Vol. 127, No 2 (June, 1994).

Limet, H. 'The Cuisine of Ancient Sumer', *The Biblical Archaeologist,* Vol. 50, No. 3 (September, 1987).

Lin, S., Sharpe, R., and Janick, J. 'Loquat: Botany and Horticulture'

Horticultural Reviews, Vol. 23, 2010.

Linnaeus, C. *Species plantarum* (Stockholm: Laurentius Salvius, 1753).

Lodwick, Dr. Lisa. '"The debatable territory where geology and archaeology meet": reassessing the early archaeobotanical work of Clement Reid and Arthur Lyell at Roman Silchester', *Journal of Human Palaeoecology*, 22 (1), (2016)..

Loyn, H.R. and Percival, J. (trs). *The Reign of Charlemagne. Documents on Carolingian Government and Administration* (London: Arnold, 1975).

Marinval, P. 'Étude carpologique d'offrandes alimentaires végétales dans les sépultures gallo-romaines: réflexions préliminaires,' in *Monde des morts, monde des vivants en Gaule rurale* (Tours: Fédération pour l'édition de la Revue archéologique du Centre de la France, 1993).

Mascall, L. *A Booke of the Arte and maner how to Plant and Graffe all sortes of trees* (London: John Wight, 1575).

Mauduit, Vicomte de. *They Can't Ration These* (London: Michael Joseph, 1940).

May, Robert. *The Accomplisht Cook: Or, the Art and Mystery of Cookery* (London: Prospect Books, 2010).

Mazzanti, M.B., Bosi, G., Mercuri, A.M., Accorsi, C.A., Guarnieri, C. 'Plant use in a city in Northern Italy during the late Mediaeval and Renaissance periods: results of the archaeobotanical investigation of "The Mirror Pit" (14th–15th century A.D.) in Ferrara', *Vegetation History and Archaeobotany* (2005) 14:442–452.

McFadden, C. *Healthy Fruit Desserts* (London: Little, Brown & Co., 1996).

McGourty, F. *1200 Trees and Shrubs: Where to Buy Them* (New York: Brooklyn Botanic Garden, 1970).

McMorland Hunter, J. and Kelly, C. *Orchard: Growing and Cooking Fruit from your Garden* (London: Pavilion Books, 2019).

McMorland Hunter, J. and Dunster, S. *Quinces: Growing and Cooking* (London: Prospect Books, 2014).

McMahon, B. *The American Gardener's Calendar* (Philadelphia: Graves, 1806).

Morgan, J. and Richards, A. *The Book of Apples* (London: Ebury Press, 1993).

Muirhead Little, E. 'Royal Banquets in the Sixteenth Century.' *British Medical Journal*, Vol. 2, No. 3376 (Sep 12, 1925).

Neckam, Alexandri. *De Naturis rerum,* edited by Thomas Wright (London: Longman, Roberts, and Green, 1863).

Nicolas, N.H. *The Privy Purse Expences of King Henry the Eighth* (London: William Pickering, 1827).

Ovenden, Stuart. *The Orchard Cook* (London: Clearview Books, 2018).

Pannier, L. and Meyer M.P. (eds). *Le débat des hérauts d'armes de France et d'Angleterre: suivi de The debate between the heralds of England and France by John Coke* (Paris: Firmin-Didot, 1877).

Parkinson, J. *Paradisi in Sole Paradisus Terrestris* (London: Methuen & Co., 1904).

— *Theatrum Botanicum: The Theater of Plantes* (London: Tho. Cotes), 1640.

Payne, W. and Herrtage, S.J. (eds). *Fiue Hundred Pointes of Good Husbandrie by Thomas Tusser* (London: Trübner & Co., 1878).

Pearson, Kathy L. 'Nutrition and the Early-Medieval Diet', *Speculum,* Vol. 72, No. 1, 1997.

Pelling, Ruth. 'Expert Guide: Archaeobotanical Evidence for Diet in the Saxon Period', *Wessex Archaeology,* 2012.

Phillips, H. *Pomarium Britannicum: an historical and botanical account of fruits, known in Great Britain* (London: T. and J. Allman, 1820).

— *The Companion for the Orchard* (London: Colburn and Bentley, 1831).

Phipps, Catherine. *The Pressure Cooker Cookbook* (London: Ebury Press, 2012).

— *Modern Pressure Cooking* (London: Quadrille Publishing, 2022).

Phipps, J.B. 'Studies in *Mespilus, Crataegus,* and *Crataemespilus* (*Rosaceae*), I', *Phytotaxa,* 257(3), 2016.

— 'Studies in *Mespilus, Crataegus*, and *Crataemespilus* (*Rosaceae*), II', Phytotaxa, 260(1), 2016.

Pitt, W. *General View of the Agriculture of the County of Stafford* (London: Sherwood, Neely, and Jones, 1813).

— *General View of the Agriculture of the County of Worcester* (London: Richard Phillips, 1810).

Pliny the Elder, *The Natural History* (London: Taylor and Francis, 1855).

Pollmann, B. & Jacomet, S. 'First evidence of *Mespilus germanica L.* (medlar) in Roman Switzerland,' *Vegetable History and Archaeobotany,* 21:61–68 Berlin: Springer-Verlag, 2012.

Postgate, J.N. *The Governor's Palace Archive* (British School of Archaeology

in Iraq, 1973).

Quealy, G. *Botanical Shakespeare* (New York: Harper Design, 2017).

Reeds, K. 'Dioscorides Unriddled. Dioscorides on Pharmacy and Medicine by John M Riddle, *Isis*, Vol. 78, March 1987.

Reich, L. *Uncommon Fruits for Every Garden* (Portland: Timber Press, 2004).

Rudge, T. *General View of the Agriculture of the County of Gloucester* (London: Richard Phillips, 1807).

Rundell, Mrs. *Domestic Cookery* (London: John Murray, 1806).

Saintsbury, George. *Notes on a Cellar-Book* (London: Macmillan, 1920).

Saladino, D. *Eating to Extinction* (London: Jonathan Cape, 2021).

Sanderson, W. 'The Plan of St. Gall Reconsidered', *Speculum,* 60:3 (1985).

Scarborough, J. 'Dioscorides in German and English', *Pharmacy in History*, Vol. 29, No. 7, 1987.

Schaik-Colijn, H. van. 'The Medlar: Going or Coming Back?', *Food in Motion: Proceedings of the Oxford Symposium* (London: Prospect Books, 1983).

Sheldrake, Merlin. E*ntangled Life* (London: Bodley Head, 2020).

Slater, Nigel. *Tender Volume II: A Cook's Guide to the Fruit Garden* (London: Fourth Estate, 2010).

— 'Nigel Slater's medlar jelly, and roast pheasant with apples and fruit jelly', *Guardian*, 5 December 2010.

Smith, J.E. *The English Flora, Vol II.* (London: Longman, Rees, Orme, Brown, and Green, 1823).

St. John Hope, W.H. and Fox, G.E. 'Excavations on the site of the Roman city at Silchester, Hants, in 1903 and 1904', *Archaeologia*, Vol. 59, No. 2, 1905.

Stratton, J.T. *Pomona's Lost Children: A Book of Uncommon Antique Fruits* (Westfield: Chautauqua Gorge Press, 2017).

Strong, Roy. 'The Laskett Gardens', *Prolandscaper,* 31 July 2012.

Theophrastus. *Historia Plantarum* (Cambridge: Harvard University Press, 1916).

Tipping, H.A. 'English Garden Making Under the Early Stuarts', *Journal of the Royal Horticultural Society*, September 1930.

Thompson, R.C.A. *Dictionary of Assyrian Botany* (London: British Academy, 1949).

Torolsan, Berrin. 'The Modest Medlar', *Cornucopia Magazine*, Vol. 10, No. 60, 2020.

Walsh, G.E. 'The Loquat and the Medlar', *Garden and Forest*, Vol. III, 15 January 1890.

Wellcome, H. *Anglo-Saxon Leechcraft* (London: Burroughs Wellcome and Co., 1912).

Van de Mieroop, M. *The Ancient Mesopotamian City* (Oxford: Oxford University Press, 1997).

Vavilov, N.I. 'Phytogeographic Basis of Plant Breeding: the Origin, Variation, Immunity and Breeding of Cultivated Plants', *Chronica Botanica*, 13:1-366, 1951.

Viswanathan, S. 'The Medlar in the Forest of Arden', *Neuphilologische Mitteilungen*, Vol. 77, No. 1, 1976.

Voaides, C., Radu, N., Birza, E., and Babeanu, B. 'Medlar: A Comprehensive and Integrative Review', *Plants (Basel)*, 2021, 10(11):2344.

Webster, Rev. W. 'On Certain Points Concerning the Origin and Relations of the Basque Race', *Journal of the Royal Anthropological Institute,* Vol 2, 1873.

Wild at Heart. *The Hedgerow Cookbook* (London: Pavilion Books, 2013).

Wood, B. *Let's Preserve It* (London: Souvenir Press, 1970).

Woudstra, J. and O'Halloran, S. 'The Exactness and Nicety of Those Things: Sir John Reresby's Garden Notebook and Garden (1633-44) at Thrybergh, Yorkshire', *Garden History*, Vol. 36, No. 1 (Spring, 2008).

Wright, T. and Wülcker, R.P. *Anglo-Saxon and Old English Vocabularies* (London: Trübner & Co., 1883).

Zech-Matterne, V. 'Le développement de la fructiculture en Gaule du Nord, à l'époque romaine', in *Comment les Gaules devinrent romaines* (Paris: La Découverte, 2007).

Zolnierczyk, A.K., Cialek, S., Styczynska, M., Oziemblowski, M., 'Functional Properties of Fruits of Common Medlar (*Mespilus germanica*) Extract', *Applied Sciences*, 11(16), 2021.

Zukovskij, P.M. *Cultivated Plants and Their Wild Relatives* (Farnham: Commonwealth Agricultural Bureaux, 1962).

Zupitza, Julius. *Ælfrics Grammatik und Glossar* (Berlin: Weidmannsche Buchhandlung, 1880).

INDEX OF RECIPES

Index

Tusser, Thomas, 91-2
type 2 diabetes, 108